sew liberated

20 stylish projects for the modern sewist

Meg McElwee

Editor: Katrina Loving
Technical Editor: Rebecca Kemp Brent
Art Director/Designer: Karla Baker
Illustrator: Linda Boston
Glossary Illustration: Ann Swanson
Pattern Maker: Bernie Kulisek
Photography: Joe Hancock
Photo Stylist: Pam Chavez
Production: Katherine Jackson

 Interweave Press LLC
201 East Fourth Street
Loveland, CO 80537
interweavestore.com

Printed in China by Asia Pacific Offset, Ltd.

Library of Congress Cataloging-in-Publication Data
McElwee, Meg.
 Sew liberated : 20 stylish projects for the modern
sewist / Meg McElwee.
    p. cm.
 Includes index.
 ISBN 978-1-59668-161-3 (pbk.)
 1. Machine appliqué--Patterns. 2. Embroidery--
Patterns. I. Title.
 TT779.M384 2009
 746.44'5041--dc22

                         2009008802

10 9 8 7 6 5 4 3 2

ACKNOWLEDGMENTS

With gratitude . . .

. . . for my mother, who once had a bumper sticker that said, "The one who dies with the most fabric wins." Mom, I think I just might win.

. . . for my father, who emerged from retirement to help make *Sew Liberated* patterns a reality, shipping orders while we were still living in Mexico.

. . . for my husband, Patrick, who planted the seed with the following words: "Why don't you try selling patterns for some of these things that you make so you can support your fabric buying habit?" Thank you for being a constant source of strength, wit, and inspiration.

. . . for my son, Finnian, who had the same gestational time as this book. You made my belly big and you bring me immeasurable happiness. It's easier, however, to pin a quilt with you on the outside of my belly.

. . . for my students in Mexico, who cooked with abandon in all sorts of funny looking apron prototypes before I hit upon the right ones. You taught me so much about myself, about human potential, and about the wonders of childhood. I miss you dearly.

. . . for my blog friends and readers, who are a constant source of inspiration for my creative exploits and my work with children. Thanks for continuing to stop by even during those creative dry spells that prominently feature my cats and their exploits.

. . . for my editors, Katrina Loving and Tricia Waddell, for putting up with pregnancy brain and new mama brain, and for patiently waiting for these acknowledgments to be written at a time when I spent many hours watching my newborn sleep.

. . . for Amanda Soule, who, in her kindness, opened up this door of opportunity for me. Thank you for your advice and sweet words of encouragement.

. . . for Linda Roghaar, who believed in my abilities as a writer and designer. Your expertise was key to making these ideas a reality.

. . . for the lovely folks at Purlsoho.com, for providing most of the fabric for the projects in the book. It is because of you that I just might end up beating my mother in the aforementioned friendly fabric competition.

INTRODUCTION:

WHY i STITCH

My mother was a prolific seamstress throughout my childhood, whipping up her own clothing, my holiday garb, and (in my humble and biased opinion) some of the most spectacular Halloween costumes west of the Mississippi. During this time, I was, unconsciously, becoming a lover of fabric and an aficionada of all things handmade.

Of course, as a child of the 1980s, I fell prey to the puff paint mania and the fringed t-shirt rage. In fact, the first solo sewing project that I embarked upon, at age ten, was a reverse appliquéd, fringed-"V" t-shirt and short set.

The years passed, and my interests shifted from crafting to the drama of adolescence and early adulthood. It wasn't until graduate school that I found myself perusing Craigslist.org for a cheap sewing machine after suddenly being consumed by an overwhelming urge to sew. Before I realized what was happening, I was caught up in the handmade movement that swept through my generation like a storm, bringing with it the nourishing waters of the needle arts from the past and quenching a longing for a simpler, slower, and more conscious lifestyle.

After graduate school, my husband and I packed up our few possessions, including that sewing machine I had bought, and moved to rural Mexico, where I spent three years teaching in a one-room Montessori school. During that time, I sewed everything from tiny aprons for the children and learning materials for the classroom to my own clothing and home décor. Due to the scarcity of fabric resources in our area, I would fill a suitcase with fabric whenever we returned to the United States for a visit, but my fabric stash quickly dwindled. I began designing my own patterns to find a use for all of those precious fabric scraps. Soon enough, that old sewing machine began to act up, so I started experimenting with hand appliqué, embroidery, and handsewing. I spent many afternoons curled up with a needle and thread, working those bits and pieces of scrap fabric into unique designs, which later became pillows, clothing, bags, and aprons. Suddenly, a basic sewing pattern worked up with ho-hum fabric just wasn't enough. Those little scraps always called to me, begging to be added as a special touch on a project that could use a bit more individuality, a bit more effort, and a bit more art in order to make it into an heirloom.

In this book, you will find step-by-step instructions on the appliqué techniques used along with a treasure trove of projects including garments and accessories for both adults and children, home décor, and a variety of fun and practical bags. All of the projects include appliqué elements that are perfect for using up all those bits and pieces of fabric you probably have left over from other projects.

I invite you to take your sewing into your own hands, to make it yours, and to put that stamp of love on it for future generations.

Happy sewing,

meg

EQUIPMENT, TOOLS, AND SUPPLIES

There are many sewing goodies that most of us would love to have in our sewing rooms, but since most of us have budgets, it's a good idea to prioritize and be informed. The following pages include explanations of some essential tools and materials for general sewing and appliqué, as well as a few useful extras.

the essentials

The following information on some of the essential tools and materials will help you pinpoint the necessary features or choose the correct type for your needs.

Sewing Machine

Although there are some wonderful machines available, with a plethora of stitches, here are some essentials to look for if you plan to invest in a more modest machine.

Zigzag stitch: A machine with the ability to do an adjustable width and length zigzag stitch is a must. Most sewing machines include this as a standard stitch (even very old machines usually have a zigzag stitch function or attachment).

Needle position adjustment capability: While not necessary, the ability to adjust your machine's needle so that it sews slightly to the left or right of the center position is a plus.

Retractable feed dogs: Can your feed dogs (those serrated pieces of metal that move the fabric along under the presser foot) be lowered? If not, you might consider asking an expert at your local sewing store if you can retrofit your machine with a special feed dog cover that can be added when you want to experiment with free-motion stitching.

Sewing Machine Needles

Don't forget to change your machine's needle every two or three projects! Needles come in all shapes and sizes, varying in their sharpness, eye size, and

YOUR SEWING ROOM

Here is a list of things you should have on hand before beginning any of the projects in this book. Anything further that you need will be listed at the beginning of each individual project.

Sewing machine and extra needles

Iron and ironing board (make sure your iron has adjustable temperature settings; a steam setting is a bonus)

Straight edge

Straight pins

Short pins for hand appliqué

Erasable fabric marking pen or tailor's chalk

Sewing, craft, and embroidery scissors

Handsewing needles

Seam ripper

shaft thickness, and there are specific needles for sewing on different types of fabrics.

Needle shopping can be confusing, because needle sizes are usually marked with both a European and a U.S. number. U.S. numbers are smaller and on the right (the thinnest needle you can get is an 8) and European numbers are larger and on the left (the thinnest being a 60). Always choose the thinnest needle that has the appropriate point sharpness and eye size for your project (refer to your sewing machine manual for information on choosing a needle for your project).

The next thing to look for is the letter value on the pack of needles. H–M needles have sharper points and are useful for straight and zigzag sewing on both cotton and silk fabrics with either cotton or silk thread. H–E needles are good to use with embroidery thread. If you are stitching a knitted fabric, you'll want to look for a ballpoint needle.

Sewing Machine Presser Feet

Here are some presser feet that will come in very handy for various projects in this book.

Walking Foot (a): Also called an Even-Feed Foot, it is a great investment if you'll be doing a lot of quilting and can also be helpful when sewing binding. It has two sets of "teeth" that grip multiple layers of fabric, minimizing shifting and making it easier to avoid bunching the fabric.

Edgestitch Foot or Blind-Hem Foot (b): Both of these feet come with a metal "bumper" that glides along the edge of the fabric or appliqué, helping you to make spiffy straight stitches, fret-free blanket stitches, and the blind-hem stitch. One word of caution: a blind-hem foot can do everything an edgestitch foot can, but an edgestitch foot can't do a blind hem.

Open-Toe Embroidery Foot (c): This foot is one that I cannot live without. It has a wide opening on the front end so you can clearly see the stitching and the edge of the appliqué. You can appliqué with a standard straight-stitch foot, but it will be a bit tricky and frustrating.

Darning Foot (d): A darning foot has an open (or sometimes partial) circle where you would expect the traditional presser foot. This special foot allows you to move the fabric freely underneath it, which is indispensable for any sort of free-motion stitching.

Straight Edge

A straight edge is essential for measuring and drawing straight lines. A clear, gridded acrylic ruler makes drawing straight lines and squaring corners very easy. You may also want to have a yardstick on hand for marking longer lines.

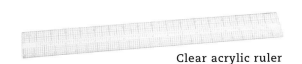

Clear acrylic ruler

Short Pins

Invest in the shortest pins that you can find for use in hand-appliqué work. Your fingers will thank you because those longer, standard-sized pins can really get in the way and cause you countless pricks.

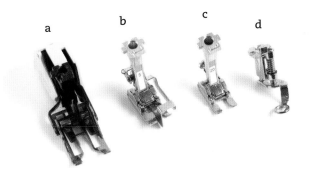

a b c d

Fabric Shears

Embroidery Scissors

Scissors

In addition to your sewing scissors (fabric shears), you'll also need a pair of sharp embroidery scissors for cutting out small appliqué shapes and clipping around edges as well as a pair of craft scissors for cutting template plastic, paper, and other materials (these can simply be a cheap pair of standard scissors).

Handsewing Needles

There are a variety of handsewing needles available. Pick the needle that feels the best to you. Obviously, the smaller the needle, the less conspicuous the hole it makes in the fabric. With this in mind, choose a needle that feels sturdy enough that you can hand-sew with confidence, but also makes the smallest hole possible. I'd start off with a handful of each of the following needle types: Betweens (the shortest), Sharps (slightly longer), Straw/Milliner's (even longer and often used in needle-turned appliqué), and a chenille needle, which has a large eye that comes in handy when you need to bring a larger, decorative thread to the back of an appliqué for a hidden finish.

Thread

So how does one identify those cryptic number markings on a spool of thread? The first number indicates the thread diameter—the higher the number, the smaller the thread is in diameter. The next number indicates the quantity of fine threads that are twisted together to form the piece of working thread. If you are lucky, the spool will also be marked with its designated use: all-purpose, bobbin, hand quilting, machine quilting, etc.

Cotton thread is widely available in a variety of colors, making it easy to match to your project. For the majority of machine-embroidery projects, you should look for 60/2 or 50/2 embroidery thread. For hand-appliqué work you'll want to use 60/2. If you desire a thicker, more rustic look to your machine stitching, choose a thicker 12/2 embroidery thread.

Silk thread is luxurious and beautiful with a price to match. It is so fine that stitches are close to invisible, making it a fabulous choice for hand appliqué.

Polyester and **rayon** are synthetic threads that offer a sheen that cotton can't, but they should be reserved for decorative stitching on top of appliqué rather than for appliqué work itself.

Monofilament/invisible thread is usually made of either nylon or polyester and is very thin. This is what you'll need if you want to try out invisible machine appliqué. Its sheen varies by brand, so be sure to pick a thread that really is close to invisible, no matter how the light hits it.

As a rule, be sure that your bobbin thread matches your embroidery thread in type and number. So, for example, if you're using a 60/2 embroidery thread in your top thread, go with the same for the bobbin. The exceptions are when you're doing a satin zigzag stitch or free-motion decorative stitching. In these cases, there's a tendency for the bobbin thread to clump up on the underside of the fabric. You'll be better off using a thinner thread in the bobbin, such as a polyester 80/2 to 120/2 bobbin-specific thread. Be aware, though, that due to the fine nature of these threads, you'll most likely have to adjust the thread tension, so be sure to refer to your sewing machine manual for instructions on the recommended settings for your machine. Be sure to experiment with the tension before starting on the actual project!

the extras

Although these are not absolutely essential, they are handy to have around to make your life a little easier.

Mini Iron

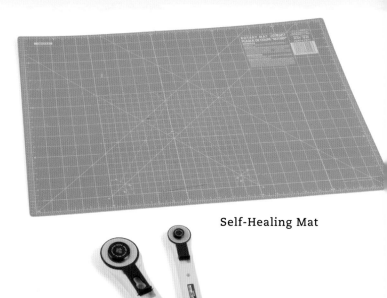

Self-Healing Mat

Rotary Cutters

Mini Iron

This little contraption, available at most local fabric stores, comes in handy when turning under the edges of smaller appliqué projects. Of course, you could always use the standard-sized iron, but it can get rather cumbersome for small, delicate work. Whatever iron you have on hand, be sure to use a nonstick appliqué mat or parchment paper on your ironing board whenever you are working with fusible web.

Nonstick Appliqué Mat

If you don't protect your ironing board while working with fusible web, you are doomed to coat it with sticky gunk—a bad thing when you consider that this gunk is likely to stick to any future fabric you iron on your board. Either pick up a special mat made specifically for appliqué work or simply grab a piece of parchment paper. Here's another trick—to keep your iron from accumulating gunk, use a piece of parchment paper on top of your appliqué as well, forming a barrier between the iron and the fabric.

Rotary Cutter and Self-Healing Mat

Rotary cutters are available in a variety of sizes, and feature a sharp, rolling blade that makes cutting out fabric a snap, especially when you are cutting multiple pieces for patchwork or squaring up (p. 156) a quilt. Use a self-healing mat underneath your fabric to protect both your work surface and cutting blade. Although it might take a bit of practice at first, I'm sure you'll soon find yourself wondering how you ever survived without these tools.

Thimbles

After lots of pushing the needle through several layers of fabric while hand-appliquéing, you might find that your finger develops a sensitive spot. You can remedy this by experimenting with various kinds of thimbles or thimble pads (small leather pads) in order to protect the sensitive area.

Thimble

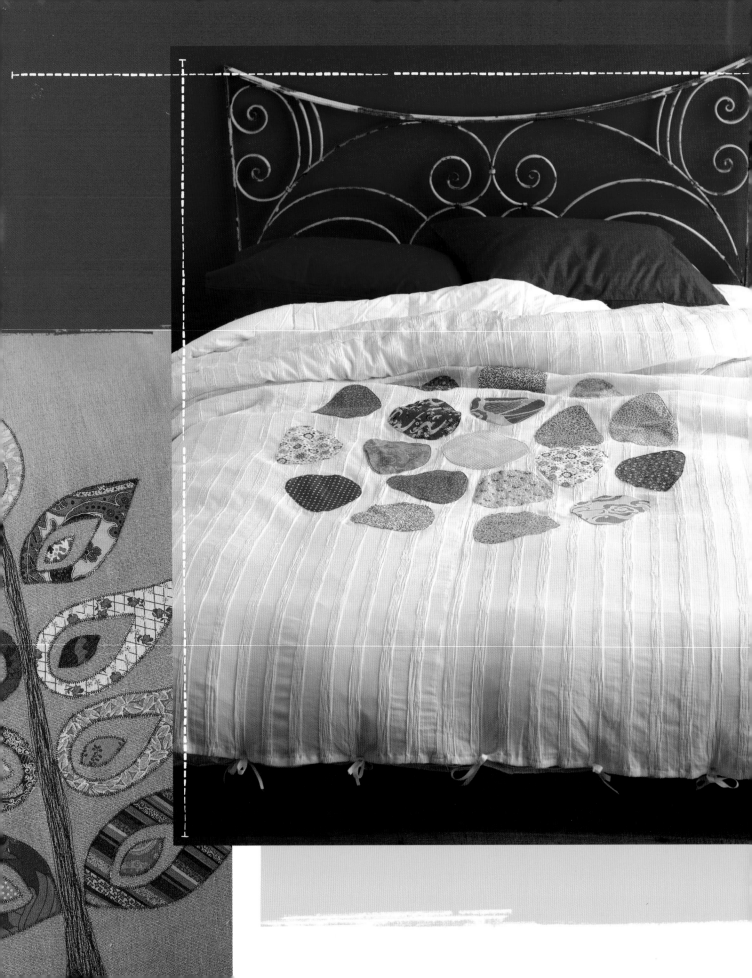

DOMESTIC ART

PROJECTS FOR MAKING A HOUSE A HOME

there's something about peppering your home with handsewn projects—it's like wrapping yourself in a cherished heirloom quilt while wearing a pair of handknitted socks. The luxury of surrounding yourself with handmade goods, however, doesn't mean that you have to sacrifice style. Go ahead—make the flirty Teacup Corset Apron (p. 19) to spice up your time in the kitchen, create a conversation piece for your living room with the appliquéd Tie-Back Floor Pillow Cover (p. 27), or give your guest bed a makeover with the simple yet stunning Heirloom Duvet Cover (p. 43).

MATERIALS

For 2 placemats

7 yd (6.4 m) of jelly roll strips or other 2½" (6.5 cm)-wide fabric strips of various lengths for placemat fronts

1 yd (91.5 cm) of medium-weight cotton or cotton/linen blend for placemat backs, binding, and leaf appliqués (at least 45" [114.5 cm] wide)

Patchwork Placemat Leaf template (on pattern insert at back of book) and materials listed under the Dimensional Shapes method on p. 144

2 rectangles of low-loft cotton batting, each 20" × 15" (51 × 38 cm)

Coordinating sewing thread

TOOLS

Bent-arm (quilting) safety pins

Walking foot for sewing machine

PATCHWORK
Placemats

These quilted patchwork placemats make for sturdy, everyday table use. Make a set of two for Saturday morning waffles in the breakfast nook, or sew up a complete set to bedeck the Thanksgiving table. The patchwork adds color while the pretty leaf appliqué adds a charming sophistication that is sure to enhance your dining experience.

FINISHED SIZE
Placemat is 18½" × 13" (47 × 33 cm).

PATCHWORK PLACEMATS

Cut the Fabric

1 From the cotton or cotton/linen blend fabric, cut the following pieces.

 2 Placemat Backs: 20" × 15" (51 × 38 cm)

 5 Binding strips: 3" (7.5 cm) wide and cut across the entire fabric width

Make the Placemat Fronts

2 Prepare the templates and then cut out and prepare two Leaf appliqués according to the instructions under the Dimensional Shapes method on p. 144. Add "veins" to each leaf, as instructed. Set aside the completed leaves for now.

3 Cut your jelly roll strips into varying lengths, each less than 10" (25.5 cm) long. Stack the cut strips into piles of coordinating colors.

4 Place two contrasting strips right sides together and sew along one short edge. Continue adding strips in this manner, alternating piles to position contrasting colors next to each other, creating one strip about 7 yd (6.4 m) long. Press all seam allowances to one side.

5 Cut the strip into eighteen 14" (35.5 cm) lengths. Save any leftover patchwork for future projects or additional placemats.

6 On a hard surface, arrange nine of the strips vertically, side by side, in an aesthetically pleasing way (see the assembly diagram at right). Begin joining them by placing two of the strips right sides together and seaming along one long (14" [35.5 cm]) edge. Continue adding strips in this manner until all nine strips have been joined into a panel measuring 14" × 18½" (35.5 × 47 cm). Press all seam allowances to one side. Repeat entire step to make the other patchwork placemat front.

Assemble and Quilt the Placemats

7 Lay one of the Placemat Backs on a flat surface, right side down. Place one of the 20" × 15" (51 × 38 cm) rectangles of batting on top, then center one of the patchwork placemat fronts on the batting, right side up. The placemat front will be slightly smaller than the other layers. Use bent-arm safety pins to secure all three layers together by pinning in rows; make sure there is at least one safety pin every 6" (15 cm).

8 Using a walking foot, stitch in the ditch (p. 153) of each long seam between patchwork strips with a straight stitch (p. 153). Begin quilting in the middle of the placemat and work out toward the side (short) edges. Sew a line of quilting about ¼" (6 mm) from the shorter side edges of the placemat as well, making it easier to attach the binding.

9 Follow the instructions under Squaring Up on p. 156 to square up the edges of the placemat to a uniform 18½" × 13" (47 × 33 cm) size.

10 Repeat Steps 7–9 to assemble and quilt the second placemat.

Finishing

11 Position one Leaf appliqué near the center of one placemat front. Use a straight stitch to attach the appliqué to the placemat, sewing around the edge of the leaf, ¹⁄₁₆–⅛" (2–3 mm) from the edge. Repeat to attach the remaining Leaf appliqué to the second placemat.

12 Make double-fold binding from the five cotton or cotton/linen blend strips cut in Step 1, according to the instructions under Double-Fold Binding on p. 154. Bind the edges of the placemats according to the instructions for Attaching Binding with Mitered Corners on p. 155.

Tip

One jelly roll is enough to make up to six placemats, so keep going and make one for each place setting!

MATERIALS

All fabrics should be at least 45" (114.5 cm) wide.

⅝ yd (57.5 cm) of cotton print for skirt (A)

1½ yd (1.4 m) of cotton print (non-directional) for bodice, neck straps, ties, skirt ruffle, and pockets (B)

⅝" yd (57.5 cm) of cotton print (non-directional) for waistband, bodice ruffle, and skirt accent band (C)

2 yd (1.8 m) of coordinating ¼" (6 mm) or ⅜" (1 cm) wide double-fold bias binding

4 large eyelets and eyelet installation tool (can usually be bought together as a kit)

Fabric scraps for appliqué (see Teacup Corset Apron templates on pattern insert)

Cotton embroidery floss in brown and white

Coordinating sewing thread

Swedish tracing paper (see Resources on p. 158) or other pattern paper (such as butcher paper or newsprint)

TOOLS

Teacup Corset Apron pattern pieces (on pattern insert at back of book; Left/Right Bodice, Left/Right Neck Strap, and Pocket)

Teacup templates (on pattern insert) and materials listed under the Paper-Backed Fusible Web method on p. 136

Serger or pinking shears (optional)

Point turner (optional)

TEACUP CORSET
Apron

Everyone should have a cute apron–not only does it make you feel great, it encourages you to get into the kitchen and whip up something yummy! This little number is one-of-a-kind. It has a unique corset closure in the back for an easily adjustable fit. Add the darling teacup to one of the pockets and you'll be motivated to take that moment to have a cup yourself in the midst of a busy day.

FINISHED SIZE
One size fits all; 25–45" (63.5–114 cm) waist circumference with adjustable ties. 21" (53.5 cm) length from waist.

NOTES

All seam allowances are ½" (1.3 cm) unless otherwise indicated.

Be sure to wash, dry, and press all fabric before cutting to prevent further shrinkage with subsequent washings.

Refer to the Pattern Guide on p. 157 for assistance with using patterns.

healthy COOKIES

These extra large, energy-packed cookies make a perfect after-sewing treat!

Yield: About 12 cookies

Time to make: About 30 min

Ingredients:

2 cups oats	½ tsp. ground nutmeg
1 cup whole wheat flour	1½ tsp. ground ginger
⅓ cup raisins	½ tsp. baking powder
½ cup unsalted peanuts	pinch of salt
1 cup brown sugar	¾ cup sunflower oil
1½ tsp. ground cinnamon	¾–1 cup milk or water

Directions:

Preheat the oven to 400°. Mix the dry ingredients in a large bowl. Add the oil and mix well. Stir in enough milk or water to make a firm mixture. Place heaped spoonfuls on an oiled baking tray and flatten them into 3" (7.5 cm) rounds. Bake for 10 minutes or until golden at the edges. Cool on a rack.

TEACUP CORSET APRON

1 Trace the pattern pieces onto Swedish tracing paper or other pattern paper, transferring all pattern markings, and cut out.

Cut the Fabric

2 Cut the following pieces as directed (using the indicated pattern pieces or measurements) and refer to the layout diagram on p. 131 for assistance. Be sure to transfer all pattern markings to the wrong side of the fabric. You may want to label each piece with a fabric marking pen or tailor's chalk on the wrong side, in order to keep track of the different pieces.

from fabric A

1 rectangle: 18" (45.5 cm) long × 42" (106.5 cm) wide for Skirt

from fabric B

Cut the pieces marked * first along the lengthwise grain (p. 152), then cut the rest of the pieces from the remaining B fabric.

*1 rectangle: 53" (134.5 cm) long × 3" (7.5 cm) wide for Skirt Ruffle

*2 strips: 53" (134.5 cm) long × 2½" (6.5 cm) wide for Ties

2 Left/Right Bodice (1 Left, 1 Right)

2 Left/Right Neck Strap (1 Left, 1 Right)

4 Pocket

from fabric C

1 rectangle: 7½" (19 cm) long × 26½" (67.5 cm) wide for Waistband

1 rectangle: 3" (7.5 cm) long × 42" (106.5 cm) wide for Skirt Accent Band

2 strips: 19" (48.5 cm) long × 2" (5 cm) wide for Bodice Ruffles

PREPARE THE TEACUP APPLIQUÉ

3 Prepare the Teacup templates and then cut and prepare the appliqué pieces, using the fabric scraps and according to the instructions under the Paper-Backed Fusible Web method on p. 136.

4 If you'd like, cut out and prepare a motif from one of your fabrics (such as a printed flower) to use as a decoration on your teacup, cutting around the edges of the design and using fusible web, as before (see the photo at right).

5 According to manufacturer's instructions, fuse the saucer piece to the center front of one of the Pocket pieces, and attach using a narrow zigzag stitch (p. 147) around the edges. Repeat to layer and attach each piece in the following order (be sure to attach each piece before layering another on top): handle (layer the cup piece temporarily to check the placement), cup (be sure to cover the handle's edges with the cup and center the bottom of the cup on the saucer), teacup decoration (optional), tea, and tea label (see the photo at right for placement).

6 With one strand of the white embroidery floss and a handsewing needle, chain stitch (p. 150) a tea bag "string" onto the appliqué, going from the tea to the tea label (see the photo at right).

7 Transfer the word "Tea" from the teabag template onto the teabag fabric, according to the instructions on p. 149. Alternatively, you can use a fabric marking pen or tailor's chalk to draw the word onto the fabric freehand. With one strand of the brown embroidery floss, use a backstitch (p. 150) to embroider the word "Tea" onto the label, over the drawn or transferred lines.

Make the Pockets

8 Place two Pocket pieces right sides together and pin. Sew along the sides and bottom curve with a ¼" (6 mm) seam allowance, leaving the top open for turning.

9 Clip the seam allowance along the curves (p. 156), then turn the pocket right side out and press flat, matching the raw edges.

10 Use a machine-basting stitch (p. 152) to close the opening at the top of the pocket, about ⅛" (3 mm) from the edge. Don't worry about tucking in the raw edges

here; they will be encased in the double-fold bias binding in Step 12.

11 Cut a 6" (15 cm) piece of the bias binding. Unfold the binding and press ¼" (6 mm) of each short end toward the wrong side. Refold the binding along its original creases and press again. You now have finished edges at each end of the piece of binding.

12 Insert the top (raw) edge of the pocket into the binding and snug it up into the crease so that the binding encases the entire top edge of the pocket. Edgestitch (p. 152) along the bottom edge of the binding, being sure to catch the binding on the pocket wrong side in your stitches as well.

13 Repeat Steps 8–12 to create the second pocket; set both aside.

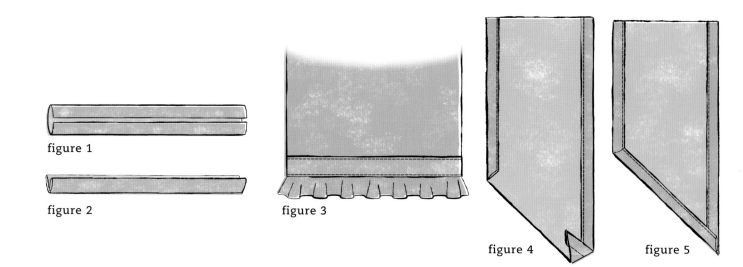

figure 1

figure 2

figure 3

figure 4

figure 5

Make the Tie

14 Lay the two Tie pieces right sides together, matching the edges, and sew together along one short edge to create a single long fabric strip. Press the seam allowances open.

15 Press ½" (1.3 cm) to the wrong side on each short end of the tie.

16 Fold the tie in half, lengthwise, with wrong sides together, and press.

17 Open the pressed center crease and fold each long raw edge in to meet the center crease and press the folds (**figure 1**). Finally, refold the tie along the center crease and press once again, enclosing the raw edges (**figure 2**).

18 Pin the folded edges together and edgestitch (p. 152) along both short edges and the folded-under long edge; set aside.

Assemble the Skirt

See the assembly diagram on p. 25 for assistance with the following steps.

19 Finish the Skirt long edges with a serger or pinking shears or use your sewing machine to finish them with a wide zigzag stitch (p. 147).

20 Press ¼" (6 mm) to the wrong side along one short (18" [45.5 cm]) edge of the Skirt, then fold over an additional ¼" (6 mm) toward the wrong side and press. Edgestitch along the inner edge of the fold (your stitching will be just shy of ¼" [6 mm] from the outer edge). Repeat entire step to hem the other short edge.

21 Press ½" (1.3 cm) to the wrong side along each long edge of the Skirt Accent Band piece. Then, fold the Band in half, lengthwise, with right sides together and stitch together the short ends only.

22 Turn the Skirt Accent Band right side out so that the wrong sides are together, use a point turner or other tool to push out and shape the corners, and press flat. The previously pressed long edges form a long opening for attaching the Skirt Ruffle in Step 24.

23 Fold the Skirt Ruffle piece in half, lengthwise, with right sides together and stitch together the short ends only. Turn the Ruffle right side out, push out and shape the corners, and press flat. Machine-baste (p. 152) ¼" (6 mm) from the long edges, through both layers. Baste again, ⅜" (1 cm) from the raw edge. Pull gently on the bobbin threads only to gather the Ruffle until it measures 41" (104 cm) long.

24 Make sure that the gathers on the Ruffle are evenly distributed and then tie the thread tails to secure the gathers. Tuck the raw edges of the Ruffle into the opening in the Skirt Accent Band by ½" (1.3 cm) so that 1" (2.5 cm) of the Ruffle is hanging below the Accent Band; pin in place. Topstitch along the bottom of the Accent Band, about ⅛" (3 mm) from the edge, through all layers.

25 With the right side of the skirt facing up, place the Accent Band/Ruffle piece on top, right side up, lapping the top (nonruffle edge) of the Accent Band over the bottom (long) edge of the Skirt by ½" (1.3 cm). Pin in place, then topstitch ⅛" (3 mm) from the top of the accent band (**figure 3**).

26 With the right side of the Skirt facing up, pin one of the Pockets to the Skirt, 4½" (11.5 cm) above the top of the Accent Band and 9½" (24 cm) from one side edge of the Skirt (see the assembly diagram on p. 25).Topstitch along the sides and curved bottom of the pocket. Repeat entire step to attach the remaining pocket 9½" (24 cm) from the other side of the skirt.

Prepare the Bodice

27 Fold one of the Bodice Ruffles in half lengthwise, with wrong sides together, and press. Machine-baste two rows down the long, raw edges as in Step 23. Gently pull on the bobbin threads only and gather the ruffle until it measures about 13" (33 cm) long. Make sure the gathers are evenly distributed and then tie the thread tails to secure the gathers. Pin the raw edges of the Bodice Ruffle to the Left Bodice at the midline (refer to the pattern), right sides up, and raw edges matched. Machine-baste in place ⅛" (3 mm) from the raw edges. Repeat entire step to make the second Bodice Ruffle and attach it to the Right Bodice.

28 Bind the edges of the Left Bodice with the bias binding. Begin by tucking the outer edge of the Left Bodice into the binding so that the raw edge is completely encased. Pin the binding in place down the entire edge and trim the binding flush with the ends of the Left Bodice. The raw ends of the binding will be encased in seams later. Return the machine to a normal stitch length setting and edgestitch the binding along its inner edge, making sure that the binding on the wrong side is also caught in the stitches as you sew. Repeat entire step to attach binding to the midline edge of the Left Bodice, including the ruffle, then repeat again to bind the midline and outer edges of the Right Bodice (see the assembly diagram on p. 25 and the

photo below for assistance). Remove any visible basting stitches with a seam ripper.

29 Sew one row of gathering stitches between the notches on the bottom of the Left Bodice, ¼" (6 mm) from the edge. Sew a second row of gathering stitches ⅜" (1 cm) from the edge. Pull the bobbin threads only to tightly gather this area, so the entire bottom edge of the bodice piece measures 9½–10" (24–25.5 cm) long. Using a normal stitch length, stitch in the ditch (p. 153) over the basting stitches to secure the gathers, being sure to backtack (p. 152) at each end. Repeat entire step on the Right Bodice piece.

Prepare and Attach the Neck Straps

30 Beginning with one Neck Strap, press ¼" (6 mm) to the wrong side along each long edge, then fold over and press an additional ¼" (6 mm) to the wrong side on both edges. Edgestitch along the inner edge of the fold (your stitching will be just shy of ¼" [6 mm] from the outer edge). Repeat entire step with the second Neck Strap.

31 On one Neck Strap, fold the sharpest corner to the wrong side as shown in **figure 4**; press. Fold ¼" (6 mm) to the wrong side along the diagonal edge and press,

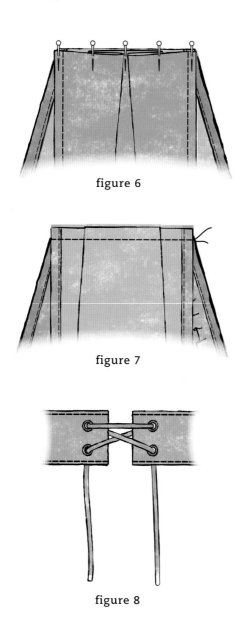

figure 6

figure 7

figure 8

then fold an additional ¼" (6 mm) to the wrong side and press again. Edgestitch along the inner edge of the fold as in Step 30 (**figure 5**). Repeat the entire step with the second Neck Strap.

32 Fold one Neck Strap along the dotted lines at the square end (transferred from the pattern), wrong sides together. Bring the two folds to meet at the notch, creating an inverted box pleat (see **figure 6**). Pin the pleat folds in place, then pin the Neck Strap to one Bodice, wrong sides together, aligning the hemmed Neck Strap edges with the bound Bodice edges (**figure 6**). Adjust the pleat folds slightly, if necessary, for a perfect fit. Stitch

together using a ¼" (6 mm) seam allowance. Press the seam allowances to one side.

33 To complete the French seam (p. 152), fold the Neck Strap and Bodice along the previous seam, right sides together, with the seam allowances sandwiched between. Stitch ⅜" (1 cm) from the first seamline, encasing the raw edges (**figure 7**). Press the seam allowances toward the Neck Strap.

34 Repeat Steps 32 and 33 to join the remaining Neck Strap and Bodice pieces.

Make and Attach the Waistband

35 Fold ½" (1.3 cm) to the wrong side along each long edge of the Waistband and press to prepare the opening for inserting the Bodices. Then, fold the Waistband in half lengthwise, with right sides together, and sew together the short ends. Turn the Waistband right side out and press flat.

36 Insert the ½" (1.3 cm) seam allowance at the bottom of the Right Bodice into the Waistband, 5½" (14 cm) from the right end of the Waistband, and pin. Repeat to pin the Left Bodice in place, 5½" (14 cm) from the left end of the Waistband. Seen from the wrong side, the Left Bodice overlaps the Right Bodice 3¾" (9.5 cm) at the midline. Angle the ruffle raw edges down so that they, too, will be encased in the Waistband.

37 Topstitch ⅛" (3 mm) from the Waistband's top edge, closing the opening and encasing the bodice pieces within the seam (see assembly diagram at right for assistance).

Assemble the Apron

38 Sew a row of machine-basting stitches along the top of the skirt (non Accent/Ruffle side), ¼" (6 mm) from the raw edge. Sew a second line of basting stitches ⅜" (1 cm) from the raw edge. Pull the bobbin threads only to gather the top of the skirt until it measures 23" (58.5 cm). Make sure the gathers are evenly distributed and then tie the thread tails to secure the gathers.

39 Place the Waistband, right side up, with its folded edge overlapping the skirt ½" (1.3 cm), centering the Skirt. The Waistband will extend 1¼" [3.2 cm] beyond the Skirt on either side. Topstitch ⅛" (3 mm) from the Waistband fold through all layers, attaching the Skirt to the Waistband (see assembly diagram at right for assistance).

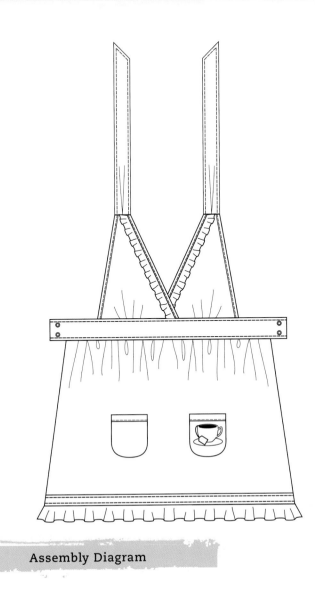

Assembly Diagram

Finishing

40 Use a fabric marking pen or tailor's chalk to make a mark on the Waistband ¾" (2 cm) from one short end and ¾" (2 cm) down from the top edge. Make another mark ¾" (2 cm) from the same short end and ¾" (2 cm) up from the bottom edge of the Waistband. Repeat at the other end of the Waistband. Following the manufacturer's instructions, attach two eyelets to each short end of the waistband, centering one eyelet over each mark.

41 Thread the tie through the eyelets as you would a shoelace on a tennis shoe (**figure 8**). Slip the apron over your head, and tie the neck straps for a perfect fit. Cinch and tie the corset straps and head to the kitchen!

MATERIALS

Yardages given are for a 26" (66 cm) square pillow and should be at least 42" (106.5 cm) wide unless otherwise indicated.

26" (66 cm) square pillow form (or desired size, see Sidebar on p. 28)

⅞ yd (80 cm) of linen or cotton/linen blend for Pillow Front (Main)

⅞ yd (80 cm) of cotton velveteen for Pillow Backs (Contrast A)

⅜ yd (34.5 cm) total of coordinating cotton print for ties (Contrast B; sample used ⅛ yd [11.5 cm] each of 3 different fabrics)

16 scraps of various print fabrics for Leaf appliqués (see Leaf templates for sizes needed)

1 package of 20" × 26" (51 × 66 cm) tear-away stabilizer (recommended: Sulky Stiffy)

Coordinating sewing thread for tree trunks and Leaf appliqués

TOOLS

Leaf templates (on pattern insert at back of book) and materials listed under the Paper-Backed Fusible Web method on p. 136

Darning foot for sewing machine

French curve, drafting compass, or a round plate for rounding pillow corners (optional)

Loop turner or safety pin

TIE-BACK
Floor Pillow Cover

A while back, I found myself drooling over a large, intricately appliquéd pillow in a catalog. Although the $150 price tag assured that my credit card stayed securely in my wallet, I couldn't stop thinking about that pillow and how perfect it would look perched on my couch. So, I went ahead and whipped up a colorful version of my own, inspired by the pricey pillow but at a fraction of the cost. Using my own collection of fabric scraps is always a sure-fire way of saving money and adding extra-vibrant spunk to any project.

FINISHED SIZE
Pillow shown is 26" × 26" (66 × 66 cm). See the chart in the sidebar on p. 28 for measurements to make an alternate size.

FLOOR PILLOW COVER

Cut the Fabric

1 Cut the following pieces as directed.

From Main fabric

Cut these pieces according to the 26" (66 cm) square pillow size in the chart in the sidebar below, or cut according to the measurements for the alternate pillow size you are using.

1 Pillow Front

2 Pillow Backs

From Contrast B fabric

Ties: each 12" × 2½" (30.5 × 6.5 cm): for a large pillow (such as the sample size) cut 6; for a smaller pillow cut 4.

NOTE: The sample uses three coordinating prints for the contrast B ties. To duplicate that look, cut two strips from each of three prints.

Don't have the right size pillow insert to make the floor pillow? Make a custom square pillow cover for any size insert! Here's a chart with the cut dimensions for nondirectional fabric:

Pillow Insert Size	Cut 1 Pillow Front	Yardage (45" [114.5 cm] or wider)	Cut 2 Pillow Backs	Yardage (45" [114.5 cm] or wider)
12" (30.5 cm) square	13 × 13" (33 × 33 cm)	½ yd (46 cm)	13 × 8" (33 × 20.5 cm)	½ yd (46 cm)
14" (35.5 cm) square	15 × 15" (38 × 38 cm)	½ yd (46 cm)	15 × 9" (38 × 23 cm)	½ yd (46 cm)
16" (40.5 cm) square	17 × 17" (43 × 43 cm)	⅝ yd (57.5 cm)	17 × 10" (43 × 25.5 cm)	⅝ yd (57.5 cm)
18" (45.5 cm) square	19 × 19" (48.5 × 48.5 cm)	⅝ yd (57.5 cm)	19 × 11" (48.5 × 28 cm)	⅝ yd (57.5 cm)
20" (51 cm) square	21 × 21" (53.5 × 53.5 cm)	⅝ yd (57.5 cm)	21 × 12" (53.5 × 30.5 cm)	⅝ yd (57.5 cm)
22" (56 cm) square	23 × 23" (58.5 × 58.5 cm)	¾ yd (68.5 cm)	23 × 13" (58.5 × 33 cm)	¾ yd (68.5 cm)
24" (61 cm) square	25 × 25" (63.5 × 63.5 cm)	¾ yd (68.5 cm)	25 × 14" (63.5 × 35.5 cm)	¾ yd (68.5 cm)
26" (66 cm) square	27 × 27" (68.5 × 68.5 cm)	⅞ yd (80 cm)	27 × 15" (68.5 × 38 cm)	⅞ yd (80 cm)
28" (71 cm) square	29 × 29" (73.5 × 73.5 cm)	⅞ yd (80 cm)	29 × 16" (73.5 × 40.5 cm)	⅞ yd (80 cm)

Prepare Pillow Cover Front and Backs

NOTE: Figures 1–3 appear on pp. 30 and 31.

2 Choose whether you will make square (pointy) or curved pillow corners. The pillow shown has curved corners; if you'd prefer square corners, skip to Step 3. To curve the corners, make marks with a fabric pen 4" (10 cm) from each corner on all four sides of the Pillow Front. Use a French curve, drafting compass, plate, or saucer as a guide—or use a good eye and steady hand to draw a uniform curve connecting the marks on either side of each corner (**figure 1**). Cut along these curves to round the corners. To ensure consistency, trace the outline of the first corner cut onto paper and use that as a pattern for the remaining corners.

3 Press ½" (1.3 cm) to the wrong side on one 27" (68.5 cm) edge of each Pillow Back. Fold an additional ½" (1.3 cm) to the wrong side on each and press again. Topstitch (p. 153) ⅛" (3 mm) from the inner folds to hem the Pillow Backs (**figure 2**).

Prepare and Attach Ties

4 Press ½" (1.3 cm) to the wrong side on each short end of a Tie. Fold the Tie in half, lengthwise, with right sides together, pin, and then sew the long raw edges using a ¼" (6 mm) seam allowance, forming a tube. Use a loop turner or safety pin to turn the tube right side out; to use a safety pin, simply attach it to one layer at one short end of the tube, then work it through the inside of the tube with your fingers until you have turned the tube right side out. Press the turned tube flat. Topstitch ⅛" (3 mm) from all four edges of the tie. Repeat entire step to make five (or three for a smaller pillow) more ties.

5 Lay the Pillow Backs on the work surface, right sides up, with their hemmed center edges abutting. Position the three (or two) sets of ties so they are evenly spaced along the Pillow Backs as shown in **figure 3**. If you have three sets of ties, position the first set in the middle of the Pillow Back and each of the other two halfway between the middle set of ties and the pillow edge. Pin one end of each tie in place 2" (5 cm) from the Pillow Back's hemmed edge and topstitch the end of each tie to the Pillow Back directly over the previous topstitching (**figure 3**). Backtack (p. 152) at the beginning and end of each line of topstitching, or sew back and forth several times over the ties to secure them. Set aside.

Create Tree Embellishments

6 Prepare the templates according the instructions under the Paper-Backed Fusible Web method on p. 136, then use the templates to cut and prepare fourteen Leaves for appliqué, cutting the leaves from the various print scraps. Use whatever combination of Small, Medium, and Large Leaves that you like; I used four Large Leaves (two for the bottom of each tree), six Medium Leaves (four on one tree, two on the other), and six Small Leaves (three for the top of each tree).

7 Leave the fusible web paper backing on the Leaves and arrange them on the Pillow Front as desired, or use the photograph of the finished floor pillow on p. 26 as a guide for placement. Allow space between each pair of Leaves to add the tree trunk in Step 9; begin with ⅝" (1.5 cm) between the lowest pair on the large tree and

figure 1

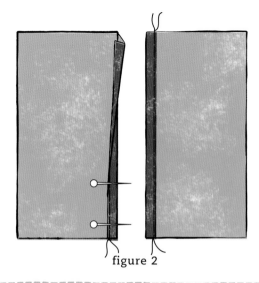

figure 2

½" (1.3 cm) between the small tree's lowest pair; taper to a scant ¼" (6 mm) at the base of the top Leaf on each tree (see the photo at left). Remove the paper backing and then fuse each Leaf in place, following manufacturer's instructions. Machine-appliqué along the edge of each Leaf using a small zigzag stitch (see p. 147).

8 Once your Leaves are appliquéd, cut a 25" (63.5 cm) long × 10" (25.5 cm) wide piece of tear-away stabilizer and pin it to the wrong side of the Pillow Front by pinning around its edges, placing it centered under the leaves of one tree. Pin with the right side of the Pillow Front facing up so that the pins are on the front, positioning them away from the area to be stitched so they hold the stabilizer securely without interfering with the stitches. Make sure that the stabilizer hangs off the bottom of the Pillow Front, where the base of the tree trunk will be. The stabilizer eliminates most pulling and puckering while you are free-form stitching.

9 With a fabric marking pen or tailor's chalk, draw the outline of a tree trunk on the front of the pillow between the leaf appliqués. To fill in the tree trunk, drop the feed dogs on your machine, attach the darning foot (refer to your sewing machine manual and/or the presser foot manufacturer's instructions for information on machine settings), and "scribble" with the thread, using a free-form motion to completely fill in the trunk (you will be guiding the fabric around with your fingers in a free-form motion, moving it under the needle as desired). If this is your first experience with free-motion

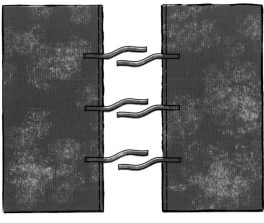

figure 3

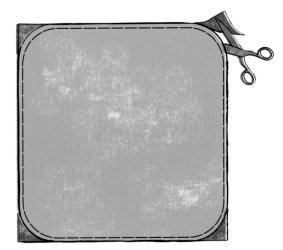

figure 4

stitching, experiment with the technique on a piece of scrap fabric with stabilizer attached as indicated above to develop confidence before moving on to your Pillow Front. Have fun with the free-motion stitches, perhaps adding "knots" in the tree or even a sentimental "carving" with your stitching. When you've finished, remove the pins and tear away the excess stabilizer.

10 Repeat Steps 8 and 9 to stitch the second tree trunk. Be sure to keep your free-motion stitching between the Leaves.

Assemble Pillow Cover

11 Lay the Pillow Front right side up on the floor or another large surface. Place one of the Pillow Backs on the Pillow Front, right side down, with its hem and ties facing the center of the pillow and raw edges matched. If your Pillow Front has curved corners, just ignore them for now. Repeat to position the remaining Pillow Back on the other pieces; the second Pillow Back will overlap the first slightly at the center hems. Flip the pillow over so the Pillow Front is on top of the stack and pin the layers together around all four edges. Make sure that you've raised the feed dogs and replaced the darning foot with the straight-stitch foot on your machine (and returned the stitch length to the default setting if necessary). Sew the layers together around the perimeter of the pillow. If your Pillow Front has curved corners, use these as your edge guide when stitching around the pillow.

12 If your corners are squared instead of rounded, clip the corners (p. 156) and then skip to Step 13. For curved corners, use the curves of the Pillow Front as a guide to trim the edges of the Pillow Backs (**figure 4**). Clip the curves (p. 156).

13 Turn the pillow cover right side out through the back opening. Press the pillow cover flat, ensuring neat seams. Insert the pillow and tie the ties. Now your pillow is ready to grace your living room!

MATERIALS

*All fabrics should be at least 54"
(137 cm) wide unless otherwise
indicated.*

1¼ yd (1.14 m) of silk douppioni for
Quilt Top (Main, see Notes on p. 34)

1½ yd (1.4 m) of medium-weight linen for
solid stripe and Quilt Backing (Contrast A)

⅜ yd (34.5 cm) of coordinating silk
douppioni for circles (at least 45"
[114.5 cm] wide; Contrast B)

1 jelly roll of coordinating cotton prints
(or about ¾ yd [65 cm] total of various
44–45" [112–114.5 cm] wide cotton
prints) for patchwork stripe and binding
(Contrast C)

60" × 60" (152.5 × 152.5 cm) square of
bamboo/cotton batting

Coordinating sewing thread

Invisible/monofilament thread for
appliqués

Coordinating cotton embroidery floss

2–3 yd (1.8–2.7 m) of coordinating
wool yarn

Thread to match wool yarn for couching

Machine-quilting thread in a color that
coordinates with the quilt top

TOOLS

Silken Circles templates (on pattern
insert at back of book) and materials
listed under Preparing a Circle on p. 142

Chenille needle for hand embroidery

Blind-hem foot for sewing machine
(optional)

Walking foot for sewing machine
(optional)

Bent-arm (quilting) safety pins

Yardstick (optional)

Rotary cutter and self-healing mat

SILKEN CIRCLES
Lap Quilt

Sometimes the fabric itself drives the design process. That was
most certainly the case with this luxurious little quilt. The lus-
trous blue silk douppioni that I had on hand was just begging
for browns, mustards, and hints of red to be added. After just
a few moments, this design emerged in my head, as if placed
there by the fabrics themselves. This quilt is the perfect size to
use as a beautiful throw in your living room and will keep your
legs warm when you curl up on the couch to read a book or
watch a movie.

FINISHED SIZE
52" × 44" (132 × 112 cm).

NOTES

All seam allowances are ⅜" (1 cm) unless otherwise indicated.

If you are unable to find silk douppioni that is at least 54" (137 cm) wide, purchase 1½ yd (1.4 m) of 45" (114.5 cm) wide silk and cut along the lengthwise grain to achieve the necessary 52" (132 cm) width of the Quilt Top.

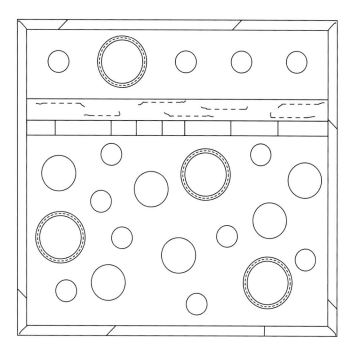

Assembly Diagram

SILKEN CIRCLES LAP QUILT

Cut the Fabric

1 Cut the following pieces as directed.

From Main fabric

> 1 Silk Stripe: 10" × 52" (25.5 × 132 cm)
>
> 1 Quilt Top: 29½" × 52" (75 × 132 cm)

From Contrast A fabric

> 1 Solid Stripe: 4¼" × 52" (11 × 132 cm)
>
> 1 Quilt Backing: 52" × 44" (132 × 112 cm)

Prepare the Quilt Top

2 To make the patchwork stripe, cut pieces of jelly roll fabric (Contrast C) to various lengths and arrange them to your liking. The finished strip should measure at least 52" (132 cm) long; when cutting the strips, remember to add ¾" (2 cm) to each piece for seam allowances. Once you have an arrangement that you are happy with, sew the strips together end to end; start by placing two of the strips right sides together and sewing along one short edge, then continue in this manner until you have acheived the necessary length. Press the seam allowances to one side.

3 Place the patchwork stripe (created in Step 2) and Solid Stripe right sides together, raw edges matched, and pin along one long edge. Sew this edge and press the seam allowances toward the Solid Stripe.

4 Pin the Silk Stripe to the Solid Stripe/patchwork stripe panel (sewn in Step 3), aligning the raw edge of the silk with the remaining long raw edge of the linen Solid Stripe. Sew together down this edge. Press the seam allowances to one side. This completes the stripe panel of the Quilt Top.

5 Now pin the Main fabric Quilt Top to the stripe panel, right sides together, aligning the raw edge of the Quilt Top with the remaining long raw edge of the patchwork stripe. Sew together down this edge and then press the seam allowances toward the Quilt Top piece. You have now completed the quilt front.

Embellish the Quilt Top

6 Prepare the Silken Circles Large and Silken Circles Small templates and then cut and prepare ten Large Circles and thirteen Small Circles from the Contrast B fabric, according to the instructions under Preparing a Circle on p. 142.

7 Arrange and pin the circle appliqués to the completed quilt front as desired, or see the assembly diagram at left for assistance. Appliqué the edges of each circle using a blind-hem/invisible stitch (p. 146) or a straight stitch (p. 146) if you prefer.

8 Hand-embroider a running stitch (p. 151) ¼" (6 mm) from the outer edge of several circles with embroidery floss; use a chenille needle and six strands of embroidery floss so the embroidery stands out. Repeat to embroider running stitch at intervals along the linen strip, knotting the thread on the right side at the beginning and end of each row of stitches. The visible knots and thread tails give the quilt extra texture and a rustic feel (see the assembly diagram at left for assistance).

9 Couch (p. 150) the wool yarn around the circles previously embellished with running stitches, securing the yarn ¼" (6 mm) outside the running stitches.

Assemble the Quilt

10 Place the Quilt Backing, right side down, on the floor or other large, flat surface. Smooth the batting on top of the Backing, then center the completed Quilt Top, right side up, on the batting. Baste the layers together using bent-arm quilting safety pins, starting in the middle of the quilt and working toward the quilt edges, pinning the layers together in rows. Make sure that there is at least one pin every 6" (15 cm) to reduce shifting (safety pins should be no more than 6" [15 cm] apart in each row, and the rows should be no more than 6" [15 cm] apart).

11 With the walking foot, quilt down the long seams between the silk, linen, and patchwork stripes using a straight stitch.

12 Using your regular presser foot, quilt around each circle in the same manner as in Step 11, stitching just outside the appliqués. Start with the circles nearest the center of the quilt and work your way out toward the edges.

13 Follow the instructions under Squaring Up on p. 156 to square up the edges of the quilt.

Make and Attach the Jelly Roll Binding

14 Cut the remaining jelly roll strips (Contrast C) into varying lengths in preparation for making one long binding strip. Join the strips according to the instructions for Diagonal Seams for Joining Strips on p. 154. Continue adding strips in the same manner until you have one strip measuring about 6 yd (5.5 m) long. Press all seam allowances open.

15 Make double-fold binding from the long patchwork strip, according to the instructions under Double-Fold Binding on p. 154. Bind the edge of the quilt according to the instructions under Attaching Binding with Mitered Corners on p. 155.

MATERIALS

8" × 10" (20.5 × 25.5 cm) picture frame (size of opening)

Wall clock kit (available at most craft stores)

8" × 10" (20.5 × 25.5 cm) self-adhesive needlework mounting board (see Notes on p. 38)

Picture hanging kit

14" (35.5 cm) long × 12" (30.5 cm) wide rectangle of natural linen (a fat quarter or ⅜ yd [34.5 cm] is sufficient) for clock face

Craft glue (such as Elmer's)

Small scraps of wool felt for appliqués: a Bird, an Owl, and 3 Circle Flowers

Scraps of various fabrics (shown: cotton prints and corduroy) for appliqués: about 78 Tree Leaves, 3 Mini Yo-Yo flowers, and 3 Mushrooms

Fusible web

3 buttons, ½" (1.3 cm) in diameter, for flowers

Cotton embroidery floss in several colors (shown: tan, brown, red, white, green, and black)

TOOLS

Wall Clock Templates (p. 39)

Template plastic or freezer paper

Fine-tipped permanent marker

Hot glue gun and glue sticks

Handsewing needle

Small paintbrush (for use with craft glue)

¼" (6 mm) round long-reach craft punch or hole/circle cutter (or size needed for your clock mechanism; see Notes on p. 38)

Serger or pinking shears (optional)

CREATIVELY PASSING THE TIME
Wall Clock

Give your sewing machine a rest with this no-sew, low-tech clock project. I love how the project lends itself to creative interpretation—it's very easy to customize. This version would be perfect in a child's room or even on the kitchen wall. Once you've mastered the techniques, try your hand at a Parisian café version or other food-related motif. You can follow the instructions given here or let your creativity run wild, embellishing as you please. The store-bought clock mechanism makes it an accessible but impressive project for yourself or to give as a gift.

FINISHED SIZE
8" × 10" (20.5 × 25.5 cm) with frame.

NOTES

Instructions on all embroidery stitches used can be found on pages 150 and 151.

Self-adhesive needlework mounting board (also called self-stick mounting board) has an adhesive surface that can be used to secure the finished clock face to the board for mounting in the frame. It is available at many craft stores and online. Alternatively, you could use sturdy mat board, illustration board, or thick cardboard and craft glue for mounting (some other types of sturdy mounting boards also come in self-adhesive options). Just be sure to choose something that will not bend with the weight of the clock mechanism because this could cause your clock hands to drag against the surface and not keep proper time.

Craft punches and hole/circle cutters are often available at scrapbooking stores or in the scrapbooking department of your local craft store. They are also available online (see Resources on p. 158). Make sure that the tool you choose can punch the hole in the appropriate place because many traditional craft punches cannot reach more than an inch or so past the border of the material to be punched. Look for one labeled as "long reach" or with similar wording.

CREATIVELY PASSING THE TIME WALL CLOCK

Prepare and Embroider the Clock Face

1 Remove the back and the glass from the frame. If necessary, place the back of the frame on top of the mounting board or other board and trace around the edges, then trim the board to the same dimensions as the back of the picture frame. The mounting board will be used to secure the finished clock face to the frame.

2 With the linen rectangle facing right side up, center the mounting board on top and trace around it lightly with a fabric pen or tailor's chalk. This will be your visible "working space"; be sure that any embellishments are inside these lines.

3 To keep the linen edges from fraying, serge or pink all four raw edges or, alternatively, you can encase the edges in masking tape. Following the instructions on p. 149, transfer the embroidery designs for the tree trunk, hills, and the numbers for the clock from the assembly diagram at right onto the working space of the linen rectangle (you'll need to enlarge the diagram to 117.5% to achieve the full 8" × 10" [20.5 × 25.5 cm] size). Alternatively, you can use a fabric marker or tailor's chalk to draw the designs freehand.

4 Using the embroidery floss, stitch the design lines, choosing the embroidery stitches according to the assembly diagram. Use one strand of embroidery floss for finer lines and use two or more strands to create thicker lines. Don't embroider the flower stems in the bottom right corner yet, as this will be done in Step 10, after the flowers have been placed.

Prepare the Appliqués

5 Trace the Leaf, Owl, Bird Outline, Bird Wing, one Circle Flower, and the three Mushrooms onto template plastic or freezer paper with a permanent marker and then cut out each shape with craft scissors. Repeat to trace and cut the Mini Yo-Yo template.

6 Follow the instructions in the Sidebar on p. 40 to create three Mini Yo-Yos, using the template prepared in Step 5 and some of the non-felt fabric scraps intended for the appliqués; set aside.

7 Apply fusible web to the wrong side of the remaining nonfelt fabric scraps for the appliqués, following the manufacturer's instructions. Use the Leaf template (prepared in Step 5) to trace about 78 leaves total onto the paper backing of several fabrics (use several green fabrics as shown or a single fabric if you prefer), then cut out the leaves. Repeat to trace and cut out one of each of the three Mushrooms, using the Mushroom templates; set the Leaves and Mushrooms aside.

8 Trace the Owl template (prepared in Step 5) onto one of the wool felt scraps and then cut out. Repeat to cut out the Bird Outline and Bird Wing, using a different color of felt for the Bird Wing to make it stand out. Cut three Circle Flowers using the prepared templates. Set all aside.

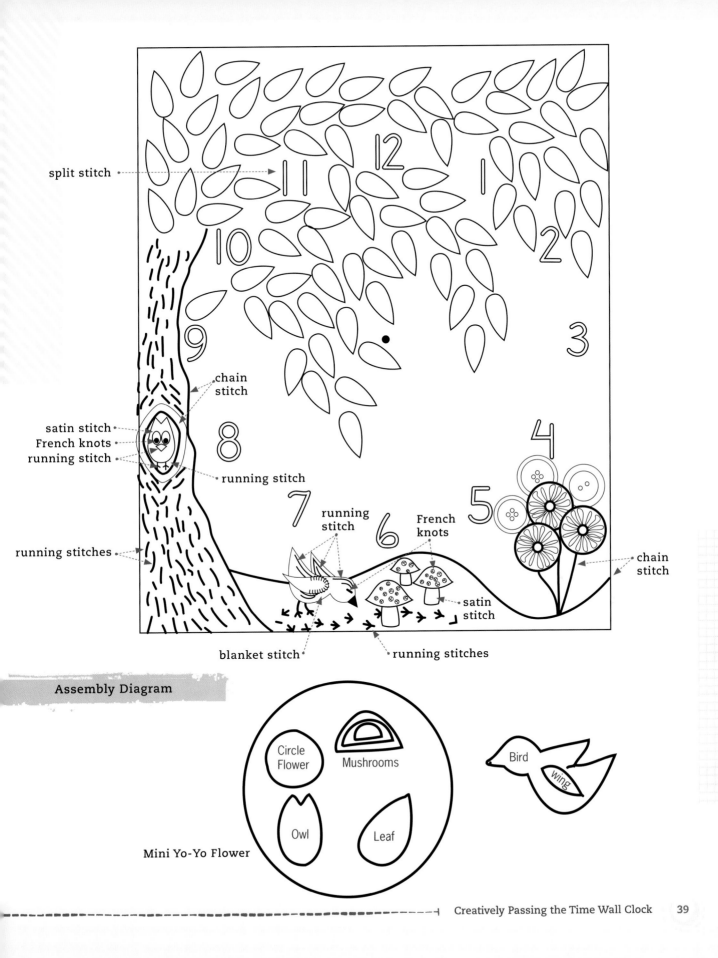

split stitch

12   11   1

10

9

3

chain stitch

satin stitch
French knots
running stitch

running stitch

8

4

5

running stitches

7

running stitch

6

French knots

chain stitch

satin stitch

blanket stitch

running stitches

Assembly Diagram

Circle Flower

Mushrooms

Owl

Leaf

Mini Yo-Yo Flower

Bird

wing

MINI YO-YOS

Yo-yos are perky three-dimensional flowers that add a stunning little detail to any project. They can be any size you wish, such as the tiny ones used for the wall clock, making them incredibly versatile.

For the yo-yos featured here, use the prepared Mini Yo-Yo template. For other projects, figure that your yo-yo template needs to be twice as big in diameter as the finished yo-yo, plus ½" (1.3 cm) for seam allowances. So, if you want a finished yo-yo 2" (5 cm) in diameter, your yo-yo template will be 4½" (11.5 cm) in diameter.

stitching recommendation: Standard hand-appliqué stitch (p. 149)

1 Place the Mini Yo-yo template on the fabric wrong side, trace around it with a fabric marker or tailor's chalk, then cut out the circle along the traced line.

2 Fold the edge of the fabric ¼" (6 mm) toward the wrong side and finger press. Thread a handsewing needle with strong thread and, with the thread doubled, tie a knot 2–3" (5–7.5 cm) from the ends. Leaving a thread tail (the ends beyond the knot), sew a running stitch along the folded edge through both layers (**figure 1**). Continue to stitch along the edge until you reach your starting point, turning the seam allowance to the wrong side as you go, but do not tie off.

TIP: To make a yo-yo with a tighter center, make your running stitches longer and leave more space between stitches. For a more open-centered yo-yo, make your running stitches closer together.

3 Pull the thread tails to gather your circle at the yo-yo center, pulling taut to gather the edges into a tight circle. To make sure the gathers are distributed evenly, take some small, hidden stitches around the gathers to secure them, then knot and cut the thread tails, hiding the tails inside the yo-yo. Flatten the yo-yo so that the gathered circle lies at the center on top (**figure 2**).

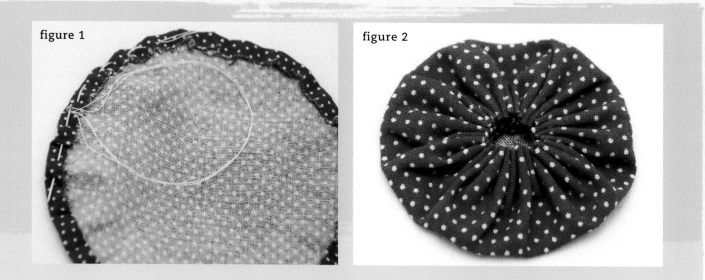

figure 1

figure 2

Embellish the Clock Face

Refer to the assembly diagram on p. 39 for assistance with the following steps.

9 Remove the paper backing from the leaves and arrange them on the linen clock face. Remember to keep all of the leaves within the marked working space. Following manufacturer's instructions, fuse the leaves in place on the linen. For this project, which won't be washed, there is no need to stitch them. Repeat entire step to fuse the mushrooms into place near the bottom center of the clock face as shown in the diagram.

10 Create a cluster of flowers near the bottom right of the marked working space by arranging the three felt Circle Flowers on the linen and placing a button on top of each. Stitch the buttons and felt in place by stitching through the buttons and felt to secure them to the linen. Now, arrange the three Mini Yo-Yos, overlapping them as desired (or refer to the diagram). Sew the Yo-Yos in place using the standard hand-appliqué stitch (p. 149). Embroider the flower stems as indicated on the diagram.

Finishing

11 Using one strand of embroidery floss and a tiny running stitch, sew the felt Bird and Owl to the clock face, placing them as desired or as shown in the diagram. Whipstitch the top of the Bird Wing in place on the Bird Outline or secure as desired. Embroider the legs, eyes, beaks, and other desired details according to the diagram.

12 Embellish the surfaces of the Mushrooms and embroider the stems, then sprinkle tiny bird footprints across the bottom of the working space as indicated in the diagram. Have fun personalizing your clock with whatever further embroidery or other bits and pieces you desire.

13 Carefully adhere the embellished clock face to the adhesive side of the mounting board according to manufacturer's instructions; be sure that the edges of the board are flush with the marked working space of the clock front. Working from the center outward, smooth out any wrinkles, keeping the fabric grain straight. For best results the linen should be taut on the board. Flip over the board so that the linen is facing down. Use a small paintbrush to apply a thin coat of craft glue

around the edge of the mounting board, then fold the excess linen over the edges of the board to adhere the linen to the board. Let dry completely.

14 Find the exact center of the embroidered number circle and use a craft punch to cut a small hole through the linen and the mounting board, just large enough to accommodate the clock mechanism's shaft. Following manufacturer's instructions, install the clock mechanism (if you don't like the color of the clock hands, paint them! If you paint the hands, be sure to allow sufficient drying time before assembling the clock).

15 Place the assembled clock into the frame itself and, on the back of the clock, hot glue the edge of the frame to the fabric-covered board by applying a line of hot glue on the seam between the board and the frame.

16 Following the manufacturer's instructions, install the picture hanger on the back of the frame. The hanging hole provided in the clock mechanism is not sufficient to hold the weight of the entire frame/clock mechanism, and any hanger present on the frame at purchase is too shallow to accommodate the clock assembly.

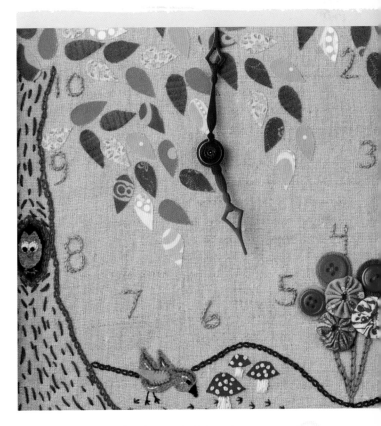

MATERIALS

All fabrics should be at least 45" [114.5 cm] wide unless otherwise indicated.

9¼ yd (8.5 m) of cotton for Duvet Panels (Main)

1¼ yd (1.1 m) of lightweight muslin

19 scraps of various cotton prints for making 18 flower petals and 1 flower center (see the Flower Petal template for sizes needed; one scrap size will depend on the size of object used to create the Flower Center)

5 yd (4.5 m) of ½" (1.3 cm)-wide grosgrain ribbon to match Main fabric

Coordinating sewing thread

Invisible/monofilament thread

Fray Check

TOOLS

Heirloom Duvet Flower Petal template (on pattern insert at back of book) and materials listed under the Lightweight Fusible Interfacing method on p. 138 (you will not need the interfacing because you will be directed to use the muslin instead)

Round salad plate or other round object about 7½" (19 cm) in diameter (or a drafting compass) for making Flower Center template

Bent-arm (quilting) safety pins

Point turner (optional)

HEIRLOOM
Duvet Cover

This lovely duvet cover features a simple, modern flower appliqué design and a deceptively simple construction. If you have family or friends coming for a visit and need to give your guest room a boost, you can easily turn out this project in just a day. Choose an airy cotton background fabric with texture or a more sturdy, home-décor weight cotton, but keep the main fabric subdued in order to make the flower appliqué really "pop."

FINISHED SIZE

Duvet Cover shown is 79½" × 82" (202 × 208.5 cm).

TO CUSTOMIZE THE DUVET COVER: Measure your comforter's length and width, then add 2" (5 cm) to each measurement for ease and seam allowances. Use the custom measurements to adjust the fabric yardages and panel sizes. If you are making a twin-size duvet cover, you may only be able to fit one row of appliqué petals instead of two.

All seam allowances are ½" (1.3 cm) unless otherwise indicated.

Be sure to wash, dry, and press all of your fabric before sewing to avoid further shrinkage with subsequent washings.

HEIRLOOM DUVET COVER

Cut the Fabric and Make the Front and Back Panels

1 Cut four Duvet Panels from the Main fabric, each measuring 2¼ yd × 42" (2 m × 106.5 cm).

NOTE: An extra ¼ yd [23 cm] of fabric is included in the Main fabric listing on p. 43 to compensate for any shrinkage that may occur when prewashing the fabric.

2 Place two Duvet Panels right sides together and pin one long edge. Sew this edge and then press the seam allowances open. Repeat with the remaining Duvet Panels. You have now assembled the front and back panels.

Prepare and Attach the Appliqués

3 Prepare the Flower Petal Template and use it to cut and prepare eighteen Flower Petal appliqués from the various cotton prints according to the Lightweight Fusible Interfacing method on p. 138. Substitute muslin for the fusible interfacing called for in the instructions (you won't be able to fuse the pieces to the background fabric but pinning will work just fine for these appliqués).

4 Trace the salad plate or other object (or use the drafting compass to draw a circle about 7½" [19 cm] in diameter) to create a template for the Flower Center. Use the template to prepare the Flower Center appliqué as in Step 3.

5 Pick one of the panels (created in Steps 1 and 2) to be the front panel. Lay it right side up on a hard, flat work surface. Find the exact center of the cover (over the seam), center the Flower Center appliqué on this spot, and use bent-arm safety pins to attach the appliqué to the panel. Arrange and pin seven Flower Petal appliqués around the Flower Center with their narrower ends toward the center. Arrange and pin the remaining eleven Flower Petals in a concentric circle around the first set of seven Petals (see the assembly diagram at right and the photo above for assistance).

6 Using invisible/monofilament thread in the needle and a bobbin thread that coordinates with your Main fabric color, use a straight stitch (p. 146) to attach the appliqués to the front panel, beginning with the flower center and working your way outward to the other petals, stitching ¹⁄₁₆–⅛" (1.6–3 mm) from the appliqué edges.

Finishing

7 On a large working surface, pin the front and back panels right sides together. Sew the long edges and one short edge, leaving the short edge at the duvet bottom open, then clip the corners (p. 156) and turn right side out. Push out the corners (use the point turner if necessary) and then press flat.

8 Press ½" (1.3 cm) to the wrong side along the open short edges. Turn an additional ½" (1.3 cm) to the wrong side on each and press again.

9 Topstitch (p. 153) ⅜" (1 cm) from the edge on both the front and back panels to hem the opening (leave the cover open; do not stitch the edges together).

10 Beginning at the outside corners, pin and then topstitch closed about 8" (20.5 cm) at each side of the duvet cover bottom, stitching in the ditch (p. 153) over the previous topstitching. This will keep the corners of your comforter from falling out of the duvet cover. Turn the duvet cover inside out.

11 Cut the grosgrain ribbon into eighteen 9" (23 cm) pieces. Using straight pins, position the ribbons in pairs (one on the back panel, one on the front) evenly along the open bottom edge, between the portions that were stitched closed in Step 10 (see the assembly diagram at right for assistance). Pin the ribbons to the wrong side of the cover, about ¾" (2 cm) in from the edge. Make sure that each ribbon is perfectly aligned with its mate.

12 Topstitch the ribbons to the cover, stitching in the ditch over the previous topstitching. Backtack (p. 152) several times over each ribbon to secure. Finish the edges of the ribbons with a bit of Fray Check. Turn the duvet cover right side out and press flat.

13 Insert your comforter into the cover and then tie each set of ribbons into a bow to hold the comforter in place.

Assembly Diagram

pampered artist

PROJECTS FOR SPOILING YOURSELF

Sometimes we crafters get so carried away with making handmade gifts for family and friends that we forget to treat ourselves to our own handiwork! What better way to kindle your creative fire than by making something lovely for yourself? Make the Bird in Hand Laptop Bag (p. 49), the custom-fit, super-comfy Jersey Garden Skirt (p. 55), or add to your bag collection further with the Dapper Day Bag (p. 75). Although I certainly advocate spoiling yourself once in awhile, the projects in this section would also make fabulous gifts. So go ahead and write that "to-make" list for birthdays and holidays, just don't forget to add a special something for yourself.

MATERIALS

*All fabrics should be at least 45"
(114.5 cm) wide.*

1 yd (91.5 cm) of corduroy, wool,
or other heavy fabric for shell (Main;
shown: brown corduroy)

¾ yd (91.5 cm) of cotton print for lining
and Bluebird appliqués (Contrast A;
shown: light blue polka dot)

1 fat quarter contrasting cotton print for
tree appliqué and front pocket accent
(Contrast B; shown: green print)

60" × 60" (152.5 × 152.5 cm) low loft
quilt batting (recommended: Throw-size
Quilter's Dream Poly, Request Poly)

3½" (9 cm) of 1" (2.5 cm) wide Velcro

Embroidery floss to match Contrast A
fabric

TOOLS

Bluebird template (on pattern insert
at back of book) and materials listed
under the Freezer Paper and Glue Stick
method on p. 140

6–7" (15–18 cm) diameter round salad
plate or drafting compass for drawing
Circle and materials listed under the
Dimensional Shapes method on p. 144

Walking foot for sewing machine
(optional)

BIRD IN HAND
Laptop Bag

Here's a cozy, padded bag to protect your laptop while you
carry it around town. The whimsical Velcro closure is cleverly
disguised as a tree trunk and the sweet little bluebirds add a
cheery touch. A wide front document pocket provides extra
storage so you'll be ready to bring your work (or play!) along
to the coffee shop or on your next business trip.

FINISHED SIZE

14" (35.6 cm) wide from side to side × 11"
(28 cm) long (not including the 44" [112 cm]
strap) × 2" (5 cm) deep (front to back).

NOTE

Seam allowances are ½" (1.3 cm) unless otherwise indicated.

BIRD IN HAND LAPTOP BAG

Cut the Fabric

1 Cut the following pieces and label each on the wrong side with a fabric marking pen or tailor's chalk to make it easier to keep track of the pieces.

From Main fabric

If you are using corduroy, it's fun to cut the Flap on the horizontal grain and the Panels and Pocket on the vertical grain as shown in the sample (see photo on p. 48). Be sure to cut and sew the Panels and Pocket with their upper edges pointing in the same direction; corduroy's nap (p. 152) causes visual color change when the fabric is rotated 180 degrees.

2 Panels: 17" × 13" (43 × 33 cm)

1 Pocket: 17" × 10" (43 × 25.5 cm)

1 Flap: 14" × 9½" (35.5 × 24 cm)

1 Strap: 44" × 2½" (112 × 6.5 cm)

1 Tree Trunk Tab: 5½" × 1¾" (14 × 4.5 cm)

From Contrast A

2 Panels: 17" × 13" (43 × 33 cm)

1 Flap: 14" × 9½" (35.5 × 24 cm)

1 Strap: 44" × 2½" (112 × 6.5 cm)

From Contrast B

2 Circles: 6–7" (15–18 cm) in diameter (trace a salad plate or use a drafting compass)

1 Pocket Accent: 17" × 3" (43 × 7.5 cm)

1 Tree Trunk Tab: 5½" × 2¼" (14 × 5.5 cm)

From quilt batting

8 Padding Rectangles: 15¼" × 11¼" (38.5 × 28.5 cm)

Prepare Pocket and Flap

Use the Main fabric Pocket and Flap pieces for the following instructions.

2 Press ¼" (6 mm) to the wrong side on one long edge of the Pocket Accent. Lay the Pocket Accent on the Pocket, with the Pocket wrong side against the Pocket Accent right side, matching the Pocket upper (17" [43 cm]) edge to the unfolded Pocket Accent edge. Sew the upper edge.

3 Flip the Pocket Accent up, away from the Pocket, and press, turning the seam allowance toward the Pocket Accent. Turn the assembled unit over, so the Pocket right side and Accent wrong side are face up. Fold the Pocket Accent over to the Pocket right side along the raw edges of the seam allowance and pin; press the new fold. Topstitch (p. 153) ⅛" (3 mm) from the bottom edge of the Pocket Accent through all thicknesses (**figure 1**).

4 Prepare the Bluebird template and then cut and prepare two Bluebirds from the Contrast A fabric, according to the Freezer Paper and Glue Stick method on p. 140 (or use your preferred method; see pp. 135–145). Be sure to reverse the template for one Bluebird so the birds are facing in opposite directions. Attach one Bluebird (facing right) to the middle of one Contrast B Circle, using the standard hand-appliqué stitch (p. 149). Embroider a chain stitch (p. 150) around the bird with embroidery floss.

5 Use the Dimensional Shapes technique on p. 144 to prepare the circle "tree" for appliqué. Pin the prepared circle (bluebird side up) onto the center of the Main fabric Flap so that the bottom edge lies ¾" (2 cm) above the bottom (long) edge of the Flap, creating a tree. Sew the circle in place using the standard hand-appliqué stitch (p. 149), taking your stitches slightly under the circle instead of right along the edge, so that the circle will look more 3D. Embellish the Flap around the tree with French knots (p. 151; see the photo on p. 48).

6 With the Pocket facing right side up, attach the remaining Bluebird (facing left) 2" (5 cm) above the bottom edge and 2" (5 cm) from the right edge of the Pocket. Use stem stitch (p. 151) to embroider the bird's legs (see photo at top right) and then chain-stitch around the bird's body as in Step 5.

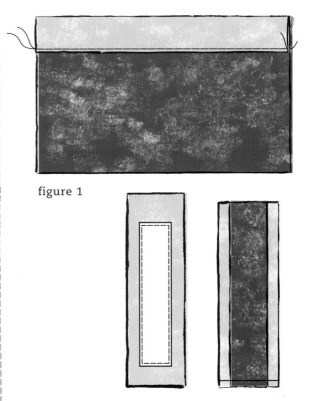

figure 1

figure 2   figure 3

Prepare the Tree Trunk Closure Tab

7 Pin the rough half of the Velcro to the right side of the Contrast B Tree Trunk Tab, centering the Velcro (side to side) 1¼" (3.2 cm) from the top and ⅞" (2.2 cm) from the bottom of the Tab. Secure the Velcro in place by sewing around the perimeter (**figure 2**).

8 Press ⅜" (1 cm) toward the wrong side along one short end of each Tree Trunk Tab. Place the Main and Contrast B Tabs right sides together, with one long edge aligned, matching the pressed ends. Note that the Contrast B Tab is wider. Pin and sew the long edge using ⅜" (1 cm) seam allowance.

9 Align the remaining long edges of the Tabs (the Contrast B Tab will bulge between the two long edges); pin and sew as in Step 8 to create a tube.

10 Turn the tube right side out and press flat, with the Main fabric Tab centered, so that an equal amount of contrasting fabric is visible on both long edges of the tree trunk, creating borders. Topstitch the pressed end closed ⅛" (3 mm) from the edge (**figure 3**).

11 Stitch in the ditch (p. 153) where the border and the Main fabric meet and then set aside.

12 With the Pocket facing right side up, position the soft half of the Velcro 2½" (6.5 cm) above the bottom edge of the Pocket and centered side to side. Edgestitch in place.

Assemble the Front Flap and Strap

13 Place the Tree Trunk Tab on the embellished Flap, right sides together, matching the raw edges and centering the Tab along the bottom edge of the Flap. Pin in place (see placement of Tab in **figure 4**).

14 Place the Main and Contrast A Flaps right sides together (**figure 4**) and pin around the side and bottom edges, being careful not to catch the Circle in your pins. The Tree Trunk Tab should be sandwiched between the two Flap pieces. Sew around these three sides, catching the end of the Tab in the stitching as you go but being careful not to catch the edge of the Circle. Clip the corners (p. 156) and turn the Flap right side out. Use a point turner or other tool to shape the corners and press flat.

15 Increase the machine's stitch length slightly and topstitch ⅜" (1 cm) from the edge along the three finished edges of the Flap. Press once more and set aside.

16 Return the stitch length to normal. Pin the two Strap pieces (shell and lining) right sides together and stitch the long edges, forming a tube. Turn the tube right side out and press flat. Increase the stitch length slightly once again, and topstitch ⅜" (1 cm) from both long edges. Press once more and set aside.

Assemble the Main Shell and Lining

17 With one Main fabric Panel facing right side up, place the Front Pocket on top, right side up, aligning the Pocket with the bottom and side edges of the Main Panel. Machine-baste (p. 152) the Pocket to the Panel using a ⅜" (1 cm) seam allowance. Set aside.

18 Place the two Contrast A Panels right sides together and pin along the sides and bottom edge. Sew along the right edge, pivot at the corner, and continue sewing along the bottom edge for 5" (12.5 cm), then backtack (p. 152). Lift the presser foot and move the fabric so the needle is 6" (15 cm) beyond the backtack stitches to leave an opening for turning, then begin stitching once again along the bottom edge and all the way up the left side, backtacking at beginning and end.

19 Trim the seam allowances to ¼" (6 mm), except along the 6" (15 cm) opening (leaving these seam allowances at ½" [1.3 cm] makes it easier to close the seam later).

20 Repeat Step 18 to sew the two Main fabric Panels together, but do not leave an opening.

Square the Bag Corners

21 With the lining still inside out, start at one bottom corner and flatten the lining so that the side seam is lying directly on top of the bottom seam. Pin the layers together close to the corner, then measure 1" (2.5 cm) up from the corner (along the seam) and mark with a fabric marking pen or tailor's chalk. Use a ruler to mark a line across the corner, through the mark just made and perpendicular to the seams (**figure 5**).

22 Stitch along the drawn line. Cut away the corner of the bag, leaving a ¼" (6 mm) seam allowance (**figure 6**).

23 Repeat Steps 21 and 22 at the other corner of the lining, then repeat again to square both corners of the shell. Turn the shell right side out and use a point turner or other tool (such as a knitting needle) to gently push out the corners.

Add the Front Flap and Strap

24 Center the prepared Flap on the bag back, right sides together, matching the raw edges. Pin together along the raw edges, then baste ⅜" (1 cm) from the raw edge.

25 Decide which side of the strap will face out, Main fabric or Contrast A. Either one looks nice; the bag shown has the Main fabric facing out. The chosen side becomes the right side of the strap. *With the bag still right side out, center the raw edges at one end of the strap over one of the bag side seams, right sides together, aligning the raw edge of the strap with the raw edge at the top of the bag. Make sure that the strap is perpendicular to the top edge of the bag, then baste it to the bag, ⅜" (1 cm) from the raw edge. Repeat from * to baste the other end of the strap over the other side seam of the bag, making sure the strap isn't twisted (**figure 7**).

Finish the Bag

26 With the bag still right side out and the lining wrong side out, slip the lining over the shell, right sides together, matching the top edges. The Flap and the Strap will be sandwiched between the layers; keep them out of the way when sewing the lining and shell together. Align the bag and lining side seams and pin the layers together along the top raw edges. Very slowly and carefully, and using a walking foot if desired (this can help keep the layers from bunching), sew along the entire top edge.

27 Pull the bag through the opening in the lining's bottom seam. Arrange the lining inside the shell, then press along the top edge. Topstitch ⅜" (1 cm) from the top edge, using a 3.0–3.5 mm stitch length. This decorative touch keeps the lining in place, and also reinforces the flap and strap seams.

28 Take four of the Padding Rectangles and stack them one on top of the other. Fold all the layers in half and then fold in half again as shown in **figure 8**.

29 Insert the folded padding through the opening in the bottom of the bag's lining. Carefully and with lots of patience, work the padding up into one side of the bag (front or back) and then unfold and arrange the padding between the lining and the shell. The rectangles should remain stacked on top of one another and should fit snugly against the topstitching around the top of the bag.

30 Repeat Steps 28 and 29 to position the four remaining Padding Rectangles on the other side of the bag.

31 Slowly and with 3.0–3.5 mm stitch length, topstitch around the entire top edge of the bag, 1" (2.5 cm) from the top edge, anchoring the padding in place. Pull the lining out of the bag and tuck in the seam allowances at the opening in the bottom seam; press. Handstitch the hole closed with slipstitches (p. 154) or machine-stitch closed if you prefer.

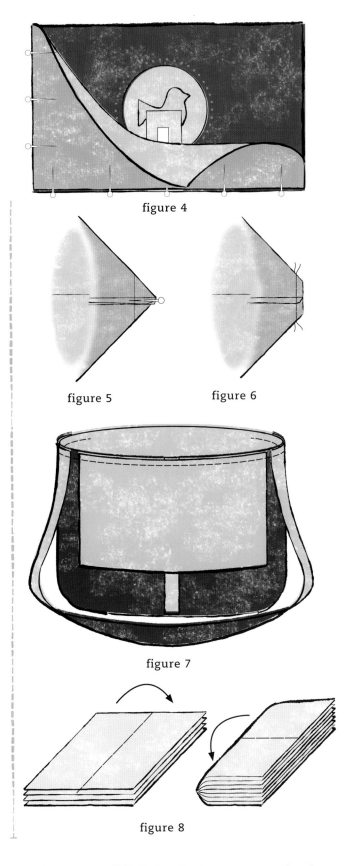

figure 4

figure 5   figure 6

figure 7

figure 8

MATERIALS

2¼ yd of 60" (152.5 cm) wide knitted fabric such as cotton jersey or bamboo for skirt shown (recommended: a cotton or bamboo blend with Lycra content; see Notes on p. 56 for information about stretch)

To estimate yardage for other sizes, calculate the length (L) [see Make Your Pattern on p. 57] and purchase twice that measurement plus ½ yd (46 cm) for the waistband and an allowance for uneven cutting off the bolt.

Scraps of various coordinating fabrics for reverse appliqués (see templates for necessary sizes)

Coordinating embroidery floss

Coordinating polyester sewing thread

Serger thread (optional; recommended: Wooly Nylon serger thread)

Swedish tracing paper (see Resources on p. 158) or other pattern paper (such as butcher paper or newsprint) for custom pattern

TOOLS

Yardstick

Pencil

Large French curve or hip curve (optional)

Serger (optional)

Jersey Garden Skirt templates (on pattern insert at back of book) and materials listed in the sidebar on p. 58

Ballpoint or stretch needle for sewing machine

JERSEY
Garden Skirt

This skirt is luxuriously comfortable and is sure to become your go-to piece for a weekend trip. I love how it can be dressed up or down, stuffed into a bag without a worry about wrinkles, and made into a whimsical artistic statement with reverse appliqué. Once you've customized the pattern for your own body, you'll have a skirt that you can sew up in a snap. You could also make a few simple, appliqué-free versions in basic black, white, and brown knitted jersey to instantly jazz up your wardrobe.

FINISHED SIZE
Skirt is made to fit custom measurements (see Make Your Pattern on p. 57). Skirt shown has a 34" (86 cm) waistband and is 31" (78.5 cm) long from top of waistband to hem.

NOTES

All seam allowances are ½" (1.3 cm) unless otherwise indicated.

See the Pattern Guide on p. 157 for assistance with using your custom pattern and definitions of the indicated pattern markings.

This project relies on the knitted fabric's stretch for its fit. Knits differ in their stretch and recovery characteristics. Choose a fabric for this project that recovers quickly, resuming its pre-stretching dimensions. To check that your knit has the proper amount of stretch, place two pins, 5" (10 cm) apart, on a crosswise fold of the knit and stretch; the fabric between the pins should stretch to at least 9" (23 cm).

Tip

For best results, give seams in knitted fabrics some special treatment. Begin by choosing a ballpoint or stretch needle that will slip between the fabric yarns rather than piercing them, which can cause holes and runs. Select a stitch that has some give to stretch with the fabric. Good choices are a stretch stitch, which moves back and forth as it sews; a narrow zigzag stitch, 1.0 mm wide and 1.4–1.6 mm long; or an overlock (p. 153) seam sewn with a serger. For any stitch, use a polyester thread, which is stronger than cotton, to resist breaking as the seam stretches. Finally, finish the raw edges of the seam allowances by trimming them to ¼" (6 mm) and sewing the edges together with a sewing machine's overlock stitch (4.0–6.0 mm wide), zigzag stitch (2.0–4.0 mm wide), or serged overlock (the serger will sew, trim, and overlock the seam in one operation). Wash the skirt by hand to minimize fraying of the appliqué fabric on the wrong side.

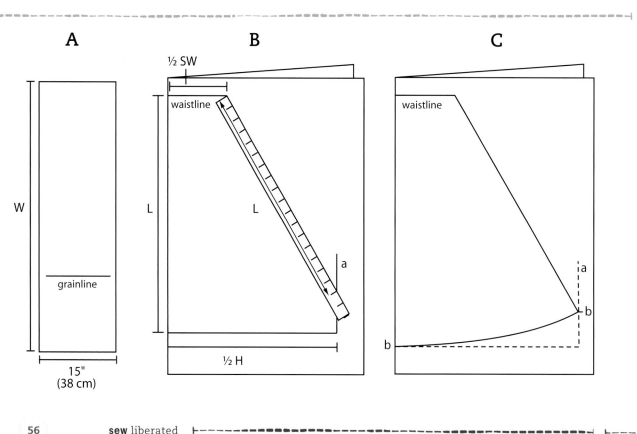

JERSEY GARDEN SKIRT

Make Your Pattern

Diagram Key:

> W= Your waist measurement
>
> SW= Skirt waist: W divided by 2 + ½" (1.3 cm)
>
> H = Hem width: W divided by 2 + 20" (51 cm)
>
> L = Desired skirt length from bottom of waistband (sample shown is 26" [66 cm])

1 To determine the waistband dimensions for your skirt, fold over one cut edge of the knitted fabric by 8" (20.5 cm) and wrap it around your waist where you would like the waistband to fall. Wrap from back to front so that the ends of the fabric come together at your front. Stretch the fabric as you wrap for a snug fit over the hips (you wouldn't want your skirt to fall off!). Use a fabric marking pen or tailor's chalk to mark both ends of the wrapped fabric where they meet. Unwrap the fabric and lay it on a table or other flat work surface. Smooth the fabric, patting and arranging it so the grain is straight and the fabric is not stretched. Measure between the two marks, then add 1" (2.5 cm) for seam allowance. Write down this measurement and mark as "W" (for waist).

2 Draw your waistband pattern onto the tracing or pattern paper. Using the yardstick and pencil, draw a rectangle that is 15" (38 cm) high × W long (see diagram A at left). Add a grainline (p. 152) by drawing a line through the pattern, parallel to one of the 15" (38 cm) edges.

3 Draw the skirt pattern on another piece of tracing or pattern paper, referring to diagram B and the diagram key above. Cut a rectangle of pattern paper at least 3" (7.5 cm) longer than the L measurement and 3" (7.5 cm) wider than the H measurement and fold it in half lengthwise. Measure and make two marks on the fold, L distance apart. One mark will be the waist; draw a line half of the SW measurement long and perpendicular to the fold at this mark. The second mark represents the bottom of the skirt; draw a line half of the H measurement long and perpendicular to the fold at the second mark. Draw another line perpendicular to the skirt bottom line through its end, extending upward toward the waistline (marked a on the diagram). Place one end of the yardstick at the end of the waistline, angling it down toward the end of the bottom line. Adjust the yardstick angle until the measurement L mark on the yardstick touches the line a on diagram C perpendicular to the skirt bottom and make a mark. This represents the bottom of the skirt side seam. With a ruler, draw ½" (1.3 cm) long lines (marked b on diagram C) perpendicular to the center fold and the side seam at their bottom ends. Connect these two short lines with a gently curving line for the skirt hem (use a French curve or hip curve to aid in marking the curved line if you prefer; refer to diagram C). Cut out the pattern through both layers, unfold, and mark a grainline along the crease in the center of the pattern paper. Mark a notch (p. 152) where the crease intersects the waistline to indicate the center front/back.

Cut the Fabric

4 Cut one waistband and two skirt pieces (be sure to place both pattern pieces with the top edges facing the same direction on the fabric to ensure that the nap [p. 152] is running in the same direction on all pieces). Be sure to transfer the notches to mark the center line on each skirt piece.

instructions continue on p. 60

REVERSE APPLIQUÉ ON KNITTED FABRIC

Whenever you are appliquéing with a knitted fabric, you will need to use a stabilizer behind your fabric to keep it from stretching during the process. I recommend using a self-adhesive, tear-away stabilizer such as Sulky Sticky +. The adhesive makes the stabilizer perfect for using on knits, while a nonsticky version would still shift around and would require the use of pins, which create holes in the fabric.

stitching recommendations:

Handstitches with embroidery floss (a running stitch [p. 151] creates a rustic look), or a straight machine stitch (p. 146)

TOOLS AND MATERIALS:

Freezer paper

Fine-tipped permanent marker or pencil

Erasable fabric marking pen or tailor's chalk

Self-adhesive, tear-away stabilizer (1 yd [91.5 cm] is sufficient for the Jersey Garden Skirt)

Craft scissors

Sewing scissors

Embroidery scissors

1 Trace your template(s) onto freezer paper (nonwaxy side) with a permanent marker or pencil and cut out.

2 Cut a generous rectangle from your appliqué fabric so that your template will fit on top of it with a seam allowance of at least ½" (1.3 cm) on all edges.

3 Cut out a rectangle of self-adhesive, tear-away stabilizer that is larger than the appliqué fabric rectangle by at least 1" (2.5 cm) on each side.

4 Iron the freezer paper template to the right side of the background knitted fabric, making sure that the plastic-coated (waxy) side is facing down (**figure 1**).

5 Remove the paper backing of the tear-away stabilizer and adhere the wrong side of the appliqué fabric, centered, to the sticky side of the stabilizer (**figure 2**).

6 Place the stabilizer/appliqué fabric under the background knitted fabric, positioning it directly behind the freezer paper template that is adhered to the right side of the knitted fabric (**figure 3**). Make sure that the knitted fabric is smooth and that the edges of the stabilizer are firmly adhered to the wrong side.

7 Using a ballpoint needle, sew a straight stitch (p. 146) on the knitted fabric, along the edge of the freezer paper template, backtacking (p. 152) at the beginning and end (**figure 4**). Check to make sure that your stitching has gone through the layers of appliqué fabric and stabilizer (if it has accidentally gone beyond the edge of the appliqué fabric, you'll have to rip out your stitching and try again; otherwise, you'll end up with a hole when you cut out the top, knitted fabric).

8 Peel the freezer paper template off of the knitted fabric. Then, use your embroidery scissors to cut along the inside of your stitchline through the top knitted fabric only, leaving at least ⅛" (3 mm) seam allowance, if not more (**figure 5**).

9 Flip the knitted fabric over to the wrong side and tear away the stabilizer from the back of the appliqué. Trim the appliqué fabric to within ¼" (6 mm) of the stitchline.

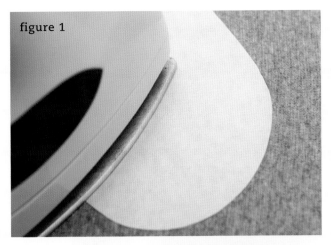

figure 1

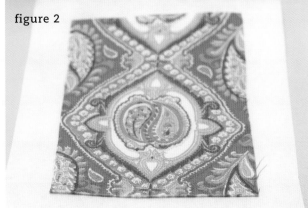

figure 2

figure 3

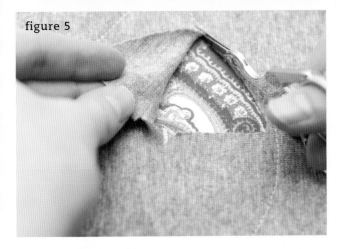

figure 4

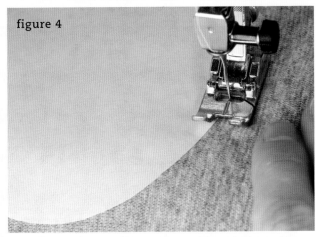

figure 5

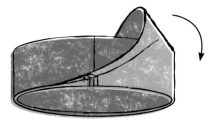

figure 1

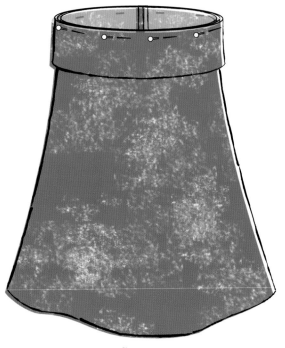

figure 2

Create the Waistband

5 Fold the waistband in half, widthwise, with right sides together, matching the short edges. Pin and sew. This is the center back seam.

6 Fold the waistband in half, lengthwise, with wrong sides together, as shown in **figure 1**, matching the raw edges, and pin.

7 Fold the waistband along the center back seam. With the fabric marking pen or tailor's chalk, make a mark on the raw edge at the fold opposite the center back seam; this is the center front. Refold the waistband so the center back seam and center front mark are aligned, and mark the raw edges at the two new folds to indicate the sides. These markings will help you sew the waistband to the skirt waist. Set aside for now.

Assemble and Hem the Skirt

8 Place the skirt pieces with right sides together, pin along the side seams, and stitch the side seams. Turn the skirt right side out and pin the waistband (through both layers) to the skirt waist (**figure 2**), right sides

together, and with raw edges matched. Align the side markings on the waistband with the side seams of the skirt and the waistband center front and center back with the center notches on the skirt waist (transferred from the pattern).

9 Sew the layers together along the pinned waist edge and then flip up the waistband. Wear the waistband folded in half, folding it over on itself. Alternatively, wear the waist band fully extended for a comfortable, over-the-belly fit during pregnancy.

10 If you are using a cotton jersey knit, you can opt out of a hem for a more rustic look, allowing the fabric to curl naturally. If you prefer to hem the skirt, choose one of these methods:

a Set your serger for a rolled hem, thread with Wooly Nylon in the loopers, and serge the skirt lower edge.

b If you are working with a ballpoint needle and a regular sewing machine, zigzag ¼" (6 mm) from the skirt raw edge. Trim the fabric close to the zigzag stitches. Press the zigzagged edge to the wrong side, turning under just enough fabric to hide the zigzag stitches. Stitch the hem in place with the narrow zigzag or stretch stitch used for the garment seams.

Embellish the Skirt

11 Follow the instructions in the sidebar on pp. 58–59 to prepare the templates and then prepare the appliqués and skirt for reverse appliqué, arranging the templates on the front of the skirt as desired or according to the assembly diagram below. Remember that the waistband seam indicates the back of the skirt. You are working with a mirror image of the final design, so remember to reverse the templates as necessary. Finally, take your time to add embroidery and embellishment to your skirt—the more embroidery, the more stunning it becomes! Refer to the assembly diagram to complete the embroidery as shown on the sample skirt. Instructions on all embroidery stitches can be found on pp. 150–151.

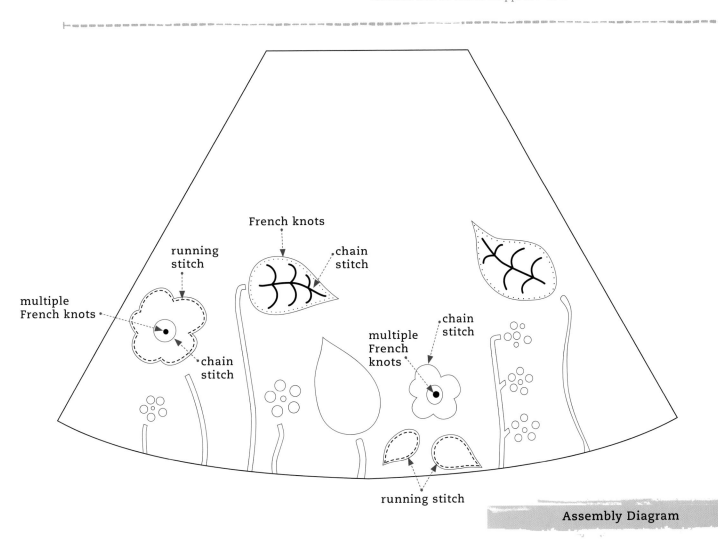

Assembly Diagram

MATERIALS

All fabrics should be at least 45" (114.5 cm) wide unless otherwise indicated.

1⅛ yd (1 m) of heavyweight fabric (shown: wide-wale corduroy) for bag shell and lining (Main)

⅝ yd (57.5 cm) of home décor–weight cotton print for bag flap, strap, and other accents (Contrast)

⅜ yd (34.5 cm) of 36" (91 cm) wide wool blend felt for padding the bag flap

24" × 24" (61 × 61 cm) square of ½" (1.3 cm) thick foam padding

1" (2.5 cm) parachute buckle

2 D-rings, 1½" (3.8 cm) wide

2 swivel hooks, 1½" (3.8 cm) wide

1½" (3.8 cm) wide slide adjuster

Coordinating sewing thread

Swedish tracing paper (see Resources on p. 158) or other pattern paper (such as butcher paper or newsprint)

TOOLS

Camera Bag Gusset, Bag Flap and Bag Flap Padding pattern pieces (on pattern insert at back of book)

Zipper foot for sewing machine (optional)

Safety pin

Tailor's ham (optional)

CAPTURE THE MOMENT
Camera Bag

Okay, I have to admit—I designed this camera bag out of pure selfishness! I needed a sturdy, well-padded bag for my digital SLR camera after having lost the simple black bag that came with it. I had a few requirements: the bag needed to have separate compartments for storing my external flash and extra lens as well as my camera body with the main lens attached; the bag also needed to have an adjustable strap so that I could comfortably switch between over-the-shoulder and across-the-chest carrying options. I hope you photography enthusiasts will "shutter" with joy after having made your own personalized, spunky camera bag!

FINISHED SIZE
9" wide × 7" high × 6" deep (23 × 18 × 15 cm) with adjustable strap.

CAPTURE THE MOMENT CAMERA BAG

Cut the Fabric and Other Materials

1 Trace the pattern pieces onto Swedish tracing paper or pattern paper, transferring all pattern markings, and cut out.

2 Folding each fabric in half lengthwise, right sides together, will allow you to cut two of the same piece at once. Label each piece on the wrong side with a fabric marking pen or tailor's chalk so identification is easy (this is very important because there are several pieces that are similar in size and shape and could be easily mixed up). Cut the following pieces as directed.

From Main fabric

4 rectangles: 10" × 8" (25.5 × 20.5 cm) with wales (p. 153) parallel to the 10" (25.5 cm) sides for Front/Back Panels (2 shell, 2 lining)

4 rectangles: 9½" × 7" (24 × 18 cm) with wales parallel to the 7" (18 cm) sides for Side Compartment Panels

2 rectangles: 10" × 7" (25.5 × 18 cm) with wales parallel to the 7" (18 cm) sides for Bottom Inserts

2 Gussets: with wales parallel to the long sides

1 strip: 3" × 32" (7.5 × 81.5 cm) with wales parallel to the 3" (7.5 cm) sides for Binding

From Contrast fabric

2 Bag Flaps

2 rectangles: 3½" × 4" (9 × 10 cm) for D-Ring Tabs

2 squares: 3½" × 3½" (9 × 9 cm) for Clasp Tabs

1 strip: 1¾" × 31" (4.5 × 79 cm) for Appliqué Band

2 strips: 3½" × 32" (9 × 81.5 cm) for Strap

From wool felt

2 Bag Flap Padding

From foam square

1 rectangle: 8" × 5" (20.5 × 12.5 cm) for Bottom Insert

2 rectangles: 8" × 6" (20.5 × 15 cm) for Front/Back Inserts

2 rectangles: 5" × 6" (12.5 × 15 cm) for Side Panel Inserts

2 rectangles: 8½" × 5¼" (21.5 × 13.5 cm) for Side Compartment Panel Inserts

Assemble the Bottom Insert and Side Compartment Panels

3 Press ½" (1.3 cm) to the wrong side on one short end of each Bottom Insert. Pin the two Bottom Insert pieces right sides together and sew along the three raw edges, leaving the pressed short end open for inserting the foam. Clip the corners (p. 156), turn right side out, and press flat.

4 Slip the foam Bottom Insert through the open end of the assembled fabric Bottom Insert. Pin the pressed edges together and sew closed with a line of topstitching (p. 153) ⅛" (3 mm) from the edge. Set aside.

5 Pin two of the Side Compartment Panels right sides together and sew a seam down one long edge. Machine-baste (p. 152) down the other long edge, ½" (1.3 cm) from the edge. Turn the panel right side out and press flat. Repeat entire step with the remaining Side Compartment Panels; set aside.

Prepare the Tabs

Note: Figures 1–4 appear on p. 66.

6 Press ¼" (6 mm) to the wrong side on both short ends of a D-ring Tab. Fold the Tab in half lengthwise, right sides together, matching the raw edges. Sew down the long raw edge with a ¼" (6 mm) seam allowance, forming a tube. Press the seam allowances open, turn the tube right side out, and press the tube flat with the seam centered. Topstitch along both long edges of the tab, ⅛" (3 mm) from the edge.

7 Thread a D-ring onto the completed tab and fold the tab in half widthwise over the straight edge of the ring, positioning the tab seam on the inside so that it is hidden when the tab is folded. Align the short edges of the tab and then machine stitch ⅛" (3 mm) from the edge, securing the D-ring inside the looped tab (**figure 1**).

8 Repeat Steps 6 and 7 to prepare the second D-Ring Tab. Set both aside.

9 Repeat Step 6 with one Clasp Tab piece, but do not press the seam allowances on the short edges to the wrong side. Don't forget to topstitch the long edges. Repeat again with the second Clasp Tab piece.

10 Thread one component (either top or bottom) of the parachute clasp through one of the completed Clasp Tabs and repeat Step 7 to secure the clasp component onto the looped tab, stitching ⅛" (3 mm) from the raw short edges. Repeat again to secure the remaining clasp component to the second Clasp Tab. Set both aside.

Prepare the Binding and the Appliqué Band

11 Follow the instructions under Double-Fold Binding on p. 154 to prepare the Binding piece and then set aside.

12 Press ¼" (6 mm) to the wrong side along each long edge of the Appliqué Band. Set aside.

Prepare the Top Flap

13 Press ½" (1.3 cm) to the wrong side along the straight edges of both Contrast Top Flaps. Center the short edge of the Clasp Tab containing the top of the clasp (the component with squeezable sides) over the notch on one Contrast Top Flap, right sides together and raw edges matched. Pin the second Contrast Top Flap to the first, right sides together, matching the raw edges and sandwiching the Clasp Tab and clasp between the layers.

14 Sew along the sides and curved edge of the Top Flap pieces, leaving the pressed straight edge open. Use a zipper foot, if necessary, to stitch close to the clasp. Clip the curves (p. 156), turn the flap right side out, and press flat. The parachute clasp should now be hanging from the center of the Top Flap.

15 Insert the two wool felt Top Flap Padding pieces into the opening at the top of the assembled flap. Tuck the felt pieces under the pressed seam allowances on the straight edge of the Contrast Top Flap and pin. Topstitch

¼" (6 mm) from the edge, closing the top flap.

16 To reinforce the seam holding the parachute Clasp Tab and to keep the felt from shifting, sew two lines of topstitching around the entire edge of the Top Flap, ¼" (6 mm) and ½" (1.3 cm) from the edge through all layers. Press the flap again and then set aside.

Attach Hardware and Assemble the Bag Shell

17 Pin the remaining parachute Clasp Tab to one Front/Back Panel, centered from side to side, with the Tab's raw edges 1¼" (3 cm) above the bottom (10" [25.5 cm]) edge of the Panel. Sew across the tab two or three times, ⅛" (3 mm) from the raw edge, to secure the tab to the bag. The Panel with the parachute clasp becomes the bag front.

18 Center one D-ring Tab on one of the Gusset pieces with the Tab's pressed edge on the guideline transferred from the pattern and the D-ring toward the short end of the gusset; pin in place.

19 Sew across the tab twice, stitching on top of the previous topstitching (**figure 2**) to attach the Tab securely to the Gusset. Repeat to attach the second D-ring Tab to the other end of the Gusset.

20 Clip into the seam allowance at the notches on both long edges of the Gusset piece with the D-ring Tabs attached. Make the clips ⅜" (1 cm) long, stopping short of the seamline. Pin the Gusset to the sides and bottom of the Front Panel. Begin pinning the gusset to one short end of the Front Panel, right sides together and raw edges matched, aligning the Gusset's short end with the top (10" [25.5 cm]) edge of the Panel (**figure 3**). The first clip will fall ½" (1.3 cm) from the Panel corner. Pin the Gusset to the Panel just before the clip, then bend the Gusset around the corner, positioning the raw edges along the Panel bottom. The Gusset seam allowance will open up at the clip to turn the corner smoothly (**figure 4**).

21 Continue pinning to the second clip, which will fall ½" (1.3 cm) before the second corner (**figure 4**). Repeat Step 20 to pin and reposition the Gusset around the corner. Continue pinning the Gusset to the Panel along its third side, ending with the Gusset short edge aligned with the top of the Panel. Sew the Gusset to the Panel as pinned, pivoting with the needle down at each corner

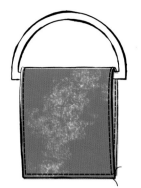

figure 1

figure 2

front panel

figure 3

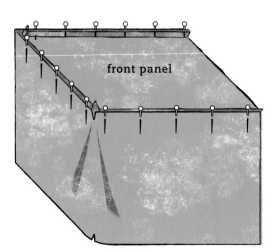

front panel

figure 4

and backtacking at beginning and end. Sew with the Gusset on top so the clips are visible as guides for the pivot points.

22 Repeat Steps 20 and 21 to attach the other long edge of the Gusset to the remaining Front/Back Panel.

23 Press open the side and bottom seams to the best of your (and your iron's) ability, using a tailor's ham or the end of the ironing board to assist. Turn the bag right side out.

Attach Appliqué Band to Bag

24 Beginning at the center of the Back Panel of the bag, pin the Appliqué Band to the bag so that its lower edge runs parallel to and ½" (1.3 cm) above the Gusset-to-Front/Back Panel seam. Continue pinning across the Gusset at the side, keeping the Band straight and level at ½" (1.3 cm) above the imaginary line between the two Front/Back Panel corners. Pinning across the bag front, ensure that the Appliqué Band covers the raw edge of the parachute Clasp Tab. Continue pinning the Band across the second Gusset side and onto the back again, stopping within 2" (5 cm) of the starting edge of the band at the bag center back.

25 Topstitch along the top edge of the Appliqué Band, ⅛" (3 mm) from the edge. Use a zipper foot to ease the passage of the foot past the parachute clasp. Once you arrive within 2" (5 cm) of where you began stitching, pause with the needle down and cut away any excess Appliqué Band fabric, leaving an extra 1" (2.5 cm) to overlap at the starting point. Turn under the end of the Appliqué Band ½" (1.3 cm) and finger-press (p. 152), then continue stitching over the folded edge and the starting point of your stitching line.

26 Topstitch along the bottom of the band as in Step 25.

Assemble the Bag Lining

Note: Figure 5 appears on p. 68.

27 Clip the seam allowances of the remaining Gusset and begin pinning it to another Front/Back Panel in the same manner as in Step 20, this time including the Side Compartment Panels in the seam. Position the upper edge of each Side Compartment Panel 1½" (3.8 cm) below the Front/Back Panels' upper edges (**figure 5**). Be sure that the top (basted) edge of your Side Compart-

ment Panel is facing the upper edge of the Gusset and Front/Back Panel because this will become the top of the bag. Pin one Side Compartment Panel to each short side of one Front/Back Panel, right sides up, then pin the Gusset to the Panels, right sides together.

28 Continue attaching the Gusset and Front/Back Panel as in Steps 20 and 21, catching the Side Compartment Panels in the seam.

29 Pin the free end of each Side Compartment Panel to the remaining Front/Back Panel, right sides up, again positioning the finished edge of the Side Compartment Panel 1½" (3.8 cm) below the Front/Back Panel's upper edge. Pin the free side of the Gusset to the Front/Back

Panel, right sides together, as in Steps 20 and 21, sandwiching the raw edges of the Side Compartment Panels in the seam as before, and sew. Once finished, your lining unit should look like **figure 5**.

30 Turn the assembled lining unit right side out to make accessing the Side Compartment Panels easier. Use a seam ripper to carefully remove the basting stitches from the bottom edges of the Side Compartment Panels. Slip one foam Side Compartment Panel Insert into each opening, tuck the seam allowances back into the Panels, and slipstitch (p. 154) closed by hand. Turn the lining unit inside out, as it will be positioned in the finished bag.

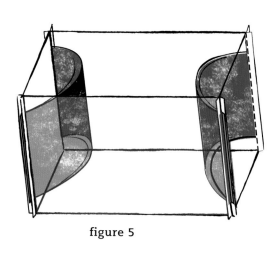

figure 5

figure 6

Attach the Top Flap and Assemble the Bag

31 Pin the straight edge of the Top Flap to the shell fabric back panel, 2¼" (5.7 cm) below the upper (raw) edge.

32 Sew two lines of topstitching along the straight edge of the Top Flap, ¼" (6 mm) and ½" (1.3 cm) from the edge, securing it to the bag shell (**figure 6**).

33 Slip the bag lining inside the shell with the wrong sides together. Place the completed Bottom Insert into the bottom of the bag, tucking it underneath the Side Compartment Panels. Arrange the foam Front/Back and Side Panel Inserts in the bag between the shell and the lining. Pin the raw edges of the shell and lining together, aligning the side seams and enclosing the foam. Sew a line of basting stitches along the bag top, ⅜" (1 cm) from the raw edge, to keep the fabric from shifting as you attach the binding.

34 Follow the instructions under Attaching Binding with Mitered Corners on p. 155 to attach the binding to the top of the bag.

Make and Attach the Strap

35 Place the Straps right sides together and sew them along one short edge to create one long strip measuring 63" (160 cm). Press the seam allowances open. Press ½" (1.3 cm) to the wrong side on both short ends of the assembled Strap.

36 Fold the Strap in half lengthwise, right sides together, matching the raw edges, and pin the long edge. Sew along the pinned edge, using a ¼" (6 mm) seam allowance, forming a tube.

37 Turn the tube right side out, using a loop turner, safety pin, or other tool; to use a safety pin, simply attach it to one layer at one short edge, then work the safety pin along the inside of the tube with your fingers until you have turned the tube right side out. Press the strap flat, then edgestitch (p. 152) around all four sides.

38 Thread one short end of the completed strap through a swivel hook. Fold 1½" (3.8 cm) of the strap over the straight edge of the swivel hook and stitch a rectangle through both layers to secure (**figure 7**).

39 Thread the other short end of the strap over the middle bar of the slide adjuster and push the adjuster up the strap. Thread this same strap end over the straight edge of the remaining swivel hook and then back to the slide adjuster, threading it under the middle bar of the slide adjuster, on top of the strap fabric already there (**figure 8**). Make sure the strap is not twisted.

figure 7

figure 8

40 Fold 2" (5 cm) of the free end of the strap back onto itself, around the middle bar of the slide adjustor, and sew a rectangle as in Step 38.

41 Clip the swivel hooks to the D-rings on the sides of the bag and adjust the strap as desired. Pack up your camera and go on a photo shoot!

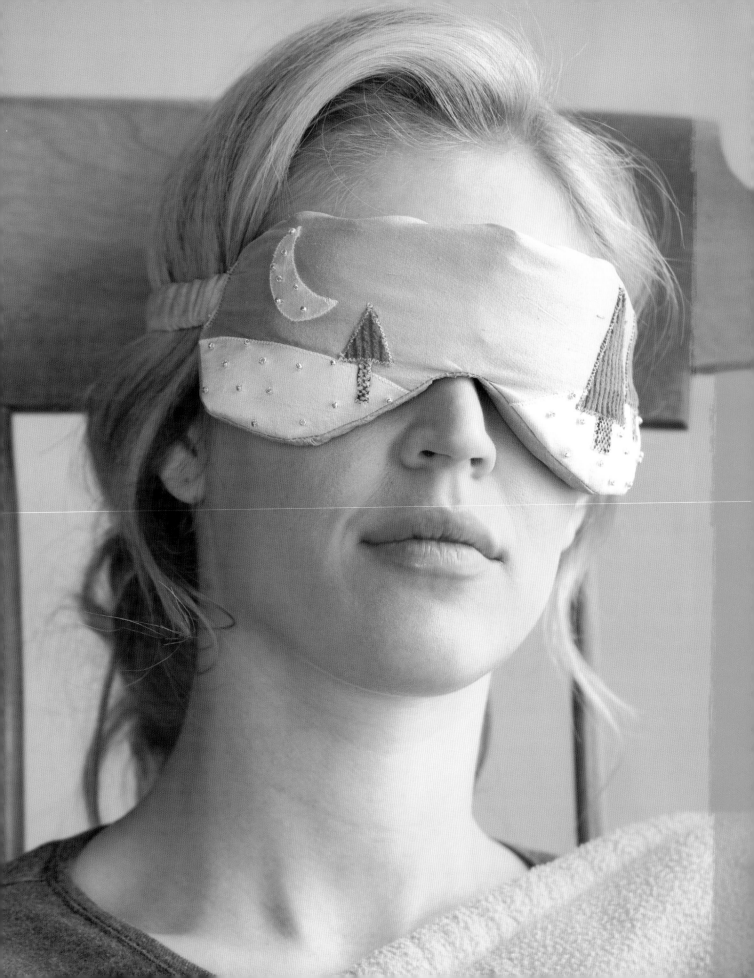

MATERIALS

1 fat quarter of silk douppioni for outer mask (Main)

¼ yd (23 cm) of muslin or other plain fabric (or 2 scraps, each measuring about 12" × 8" [30.5 × 20.5 cm]) for inner mask (Contrast)

Various scraps of fabric for appliqués (I used white silk for the Snow Banks and Moon, green corduroy for the Trees, and brown wool for the Tree Trunks; see templates for necessary sizes)

13" (33 cm) of ½" (1.3 cm) wide elastic

30–40 size 11° or 10° silver seed beads

⅔ cup of flaxseed

Soothing essential oil of your choice (recommended: lavender)

Coordinating sewing thread

Swedish tracing paper (see Resources on p. 158) or other pattern paper (such as butcher paper or newsprint)

TOOLS

Sleeping Mask pattern (on pattern insert at back of book)

Sleeping Mask templates (on pattern insert at back of book) and materials listed under the Paper-Backed Fusible Web method on p. 136

Beading needle

Loop turner (optional)

Safety pin

Small funnel (optional)

SUMPTUOUS SILK
Sleeping Mask

Doze off to the soothing scent of your favorite essential oil with this lavish sleeping mask. The flaxseed filling, paired with the soft silk against your eyes, will assure that you wake up refreshed and is similar to the headache-easing eye packs sold in stores. Plus, it's designed with an elastic band to keep it in place as you sleep. Whip this up in an hour or so for yourself or as part of a pampering gift basket for a friend or loved one.

FINISHED SIZE
9" × 4" (23 × 10 cm) with elastic band for adjustable fit.

NOTES

All seam allowances are ⅜" (1 cm) unless otherwise indicated.

See the Pattern Guide on p. 157 for assistance with using patterns.

SUMPTUOUS SILK SLEEPING MASK

1 Trace the Sleeping Mask patterns onto Swedish tracing paper or other pattern paper, transferring all pattern markings, and then cut out.

Cut the Fabric and Prepare the Appliqués

2 Cut the following pieces as directed.

From Main fabric

1 Strap: 2" × 18" (5 × 45.5 cm)

2 Outer Panels

From Contrast fabric

2 Inner Panels

3 Pour the flaxseed into a small bowl. Add about ten drops of essential oil to the seed, mix in, and let sit until you are ready to add it to the sleeping mask. This will allow the moisture to evaporate and will prevent an unsightly oil stain on the silk.

4 Prepare the templates and then cut and prepare the appliqué pieces from the various fabric scraps, according to the instructions under the Paper-Backed Fusible Web method on p. 136. Remove the paper backing and then follow manufacturer's instructions to fuse the appliqués to the right side of one Outer Panel in the following order, securing each layer with a zigzag stitch (p. 147) before fusing the next layer: Right and Left Snow Banks and Moon, three Tree trunks, and the three Trees (see the photo at right and **figure 1** on p. 73 for assistance with placement).

5 Using the beading needle and thread, handsew the glass beads to the snow and moon as desired.

Assemble the Inner Mask

6 Pin the two Inner Panels right sides together, and sew, leaving a 4" (10 cm) opening along the top, straight edge for turning and adding the flax. Clip the curves (p. 156) and then turn right side out. Tuck in the seam allowances at the opening and press.

7 Pour the scented flaxseed into the opening, using a funnel or rolled paper to guide the seeds, and then slip-stitch (p. 154) the opening closed. Set aside for now.

Make the Strap and Assemble the Outer Mask

8 Fold the Strap in half lengthwise with right sides together, matching the raw edges, and pin. Stitch the long edges, forming a tube. Turn the strap right side out using a loop turner or safety pin to assist; if you are using a safety pin, simply attach it to one layer at one short edge, then work it along the inside of the tube with your fingers until you have turned the tube right side out. Remove the safety pin or loop turner and press flat.

Tip

When sewing the seed beads onto the glistening-in-the-moonlight snow, be sure not to sew them too close to the edge or your presser foot will have a heck of a time sewing a nice seam! Sewing over a bead could break the bead and possibly the needle as well.

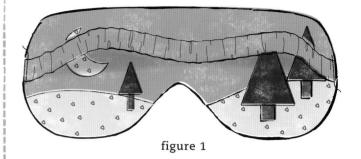

figure 1

9 Attach the safety pin to the 13" (33 cm) length of elastic and use it to thread the elastic through the tube, working it along the inside of the tube with your fingers. When the free edge of the elastic is flush with one open end of the tube, sew back and forth across the short edge of the tube a few times, catching the elastic, stitching ⅛" (3 mm) from the edge of the tube.

10 Continue pulling the elastic through to the other end of the tube, gathering the fabric along the elastic as you go. With the raw edges matched, sew the other end of the elastic to the tube end as in Step 9.

11 With the appliquéd Outer Panel right side up, place the gathered strap on top, centered top to bottom, matching the ends of the strap with the raw edges of the Outer Panel and making sure the strap is not twisted. Machine-baste (p. 152) each end of the strap to the sides of the Outer Panel ⅛" (3 mm) from the edges (**figure 1**).

12 Pin the two Outer Panels right sides together with the strap sandwiched between. Sew the Panels together, leaving a 4" (10 cm) opening along the top straight edge for turning. Carefully clip along all curves and turn the sleeping mask right side out. Tuck in the seam allowances at the opening and press. Topstitch (p. 153) a line of reinforcing stitches where the strap meets the mask on each side, ⅛" (3 mm) or less from the seamline.

13 Insert the flax-filled Inner Mask into the opening at the top of the Outer Mask, then slipstitch the opening closed. Now, take a nap and try it out!

MATERIALS

All fabrics should be at least 45" (114.5 cm) wide unless otherwise indicated.

¾ yd (68.5 cm) of medium-weight to heavyweight fabric such as wool, velvet, or home décor–weight cotton for shell (Main)

¾ yd (68.5 cm) medium-weight large print cotton for lining (Contrast)

3 yd (2.7 m) coordinating ½" (1.3 cm)-wide double fold bias tape

¾" (2 cm) magnetic snap

Scrap of fusible interfacing to reinforce fabric around magnetic snap closure (2 pieces, each about 1½" × 1½" [3.8 × 3.8 cm])

Coordinating sewing thread

3 yd (2.7 m) of ¼" (6 mm) cotton cording

Swedish tracing paper (see Resources on p. 158) or other pattern paper (such as butcher paper or newsprint)

TOOLS

Dapper Day Bag Front/Back Panel pattern (on pattern insert at back of book)

Zipper foot for sewing machine

Materials listed for your preferred method of appliqué preparation (pp. 135–145)

Flat-nose pliers (optional)

DAPPER
Day Bag

This is the perfect purse—not too big, not too small. A magnetic snap closure keeps your belongings secure and a long strap gives you the freedom to throw it over your shoulder or carry it messenger-bag style across your chest. I schlep a knitting project and water bottle with me wherever I go, and this smart little bag holds both with room to spare. Make it with heavier-weight fabric in a bold print to emphasize the easy appliqué, or work it up without the appliquéd element to put the piping and construction on display.

FINISHED SIZE
11" (28 cm) long (not including strap) × 10½" (26.5 cm) wide × 4½" (11.5 cm) deep (front to back). Strap is 34" (86 cm) long.

NOTES

All seam allowances are ⅜" (1 cm) unless otherwise indicated.

See the Pattern Guide on p. 157 for assistance with using patterns.

DAPPER DAY BAG

1 Trace the Dapper Day Bag Panel pattern onto Swedish tracing paper or other pattern paper, transferring all pattern markings, and cut out.

Cut the Fabric

2 Cut the following pieces as directed, transferring all pattern markings to the wrong side of the fabric. Label each piece on the wrong side with a fabric marking pen or tailor's chalk to make identification easier.

From Main fabric

1 strip: 30" × 3¾" (76 × 9.5 cm) for shell Top Band

1 strip: 35" × 4¼" (89 × 10.8 cm) for shell Strap

1 strip: 30" × 4¼" (76 × 10.8 cm) for shell Gusset

2 Front/Back Panels for shell

From Contrast fabric

1 strip: 30" × 3¾" (76 × 9.5 cm) for lining Top Band

1 strip: 35" × 4¼" (89 × 10.8 cm) for lining Strap

1 strip: 30" × 4¼" (76 × 10.8 cm) for lining Gusset

2 Front/Back Panels for lining

Make and Attach the Piping

3 Unfold the bias tape so the center crease is exposed. Lay the cording along the center crease, refold the bias tape around the cording, and pin closed.

4 Using the zipper foot, baste the entire length of the bias tape adjacent to the cord, enclosing the cord in the bias strip (this will create your piping). Position the cord "bump" just to the left of the zipper foot and use your finger to keep the cord pressed against the zipper foot as you sew (be careful to keep your finger away from the needle itself). To keep the basting stitches hidden in the finished project, use the machine's controls to move the needle 0.5–1.0 mm to the right (closer to the foot but farther from the cord) while basting, then return the needle to its initial position, closer to the cord, when sewing the piping into the seams.

5 Lay the piping on the right side of one shell Front/Back Panel, matching the raw edges along the rounded sides and bottom, and pin. The cord will lie toward the center of the Panel. Make sure the basting line is ⅜" (1 cm) or slightly less from the edge of the panel (**figure 1**). Don't worry about the extra piping, which will be trimmed later. Using the zipper foot, baste the piping in place along the previous basting line. At the end of the seamline, cut the piping flush with the top edge of the bag. Repeat entire step to attach piping to the other shell Front/Back Panel.

Appliqué the Bag Front

6 Roughly cut a motif from your cotton lining fabric, leaving extra fabric around the edges. Prepare the motif for appliqué using your preferred method (see pp. 135–145; I used the Paper-Backed Fusible Web method on p. 136). Hand or machine appliqué the motif, centered (or placed as desired) on the right side of one shell Front/Back Panel, using your preferred stitch (see pp. 146–151; I used a zigzag stitch [p. 147]). This will now be the bag front.

Prepare the Bag Lining

7 Pleat the upper edge of each lining Front/Back Panel, following the guidelines transferred from the pattern. Fold the Panel along each dotted line, wrong sides together, and bring the fold to meet the corresponding solid line (indicated by arrows on the pattern). The pleats will open toward the center of each Panel. Baste along the top edge of the panel, ¼" (6 mm) from the edge, securing the pleats (**figure 2**). Repeat entire step with the remaining lining Front/Back Panel.

8 Fold the lining Gusset in half widthwise to find the center. Mark both seam allowances at the center fold. Pin the lining Gusset to the curved edge of one lining Front/Back Panel, right sides together, matching the Panel's center notch to the mark at the Gusset center. Pin from the center outward toward the top edges (figure 3). Use a lot of pins as you ease (p. 152) the Gusset along the bag curves.

9 Sew the Gusset to the Panel, stitching slowly as you arrive at the curves and using your fingers to smooth the fabric as you go to avoid tucks and gathers in the seam.

10 Repeat Steps 8 and 9 to attach the second lining Front/Back Panel to the Gusset, leaving a 4" (10 cm) opening in the seam along the bottom for turning. Clip the curves (p. 156) along both Gusset seams, press the seam allowances open, and turn the bag lining right side out.

11 Fold the lining Top Band in half widthwise, right sides together, and sew together the short ends. While the Top Band is still folded, mark the center fold, marking in the seam allowance on one edge. Unfold the Top Band and press the seam allowances open at the seamed edges. Pin the Top Band around the top edge of the assembled lining, right sides together, matching the raw edges and aligning the center mark on the Top Band with the center notch on one of the lining Panels (**figure 4**).

12 Sew around the top of the bag, keeping the pleats neatly folded, and then flip the Top Band up and press flat.

Prepare the Bag Shell

13 Repeat Steps 7–9 with the shell Front/Back Panels and Gusset, using the zipper foot to stitch the piped seams. Be mindful of the piping as you sew, as it will be sandwiched between the Gusset and the Panels. Adjust the needle position as directed in Step 4 and use your index finger to hold the cord snugly against the zipper foot's left side. Go very slowly, and breathe deeply!

14 Use a seam ripper to remove 1½" (3.8 cm) of the basting stitches at one end of the remaining piping. Pull the bias tape back to expose the cording and cut the cording 1" (2.5 cm) from the edge of the bias tape. The extra fabric now left free of cording will be used to fold over and tidily encase the other end of cording once you baste it around the top edge of the shell. Fold ½" (1.3 cm) of the bias tape toward the wrong side and press (see **figure 6** on p. 78 for assistance).

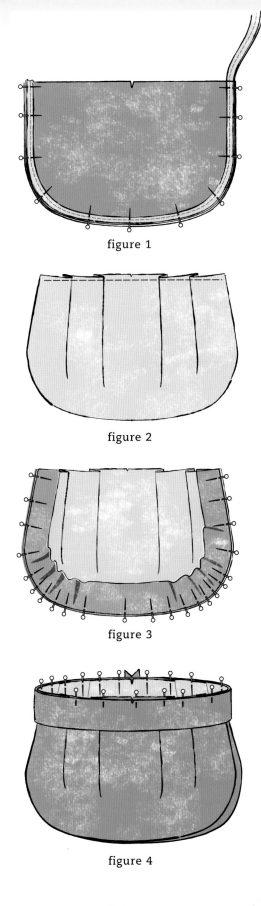

figure 1

figure 2

figure 3

figure 4

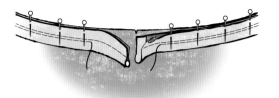

figure 5

figure 6

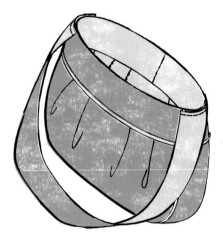

figure 7

figure 8

15 Begin pinning the piping to the right side of the shell at the center back top edge, matching the folded-under end of the piping to the center notch. Match the piping and shell raw edges, positioning the "bump" of the cording toward the center of the Panel. Continue pinning around the top edge of the bag.

16 Using the zipper foot, begin basting around the top edge of the bag next to the cording (see Step 5) and about 1" (2.5 cm) from the pressed end of the piping (**figure 5**).

17 When you are a little over 1" (2.5 cm) away from the beginning of the basting, stop sewing with the needle down and raise the presser foot. Cut the end of the piping (both the cording and the bias tape) so that the two cord ends will just touch (any overlapping would cause an unsightly bulge). Lay the cut end of the piping inside the empty bias tape at the beginning of the basting so that the cord ends are touching (**figure 6**). Refold the bias tape to enclose the raw edge of the piping. Continue basting as before until you have come back to the starting point.

18 Repeat Steps 11 and 12 to attach the Top Band to the shell, using the zipper foot and guiding the sandwiched cording with your index finger as you sew.

Make and Attach the Strap

19 Pin the two Strap pieces right sides together and sew along the long edges, forming a tube. Turn the tube right side out and press flat. Increase the stitch length to 3.0 mm, topstitch ¼" (6 mm) from each long edge, and then press again.

20 Pin the strap to the shell, right sides together (with the strap lining facing away from the shell), with the strap ends centered over the gusset at each side and raw edges matched. Ensure that the strap is not twisted, then baste each strap end to the bag, ¼" (6 mm) from the raw edge (**figure 7**).

Finishing

21 With the lining bag inside out, find the center back of the Top Band (this will be right over the seam) and follow manufacturer's instructions to fuse a 1½" × 1½" (3.8 × 3.8 cm) square of fusible interfacing to the wrong side of the fabric. Make sure the interfacing is centered over the seam and is ½" (1.5 cm) below the band's raw edge.

22 Take one of the thin metal washers from the magnetic snap and place it on the lining Top Band, centered directly over the seam and the fused interfacing with the washer's top edge ⅞" (2.2 cm) below the band's raw edge. Use a pen or pencil to mark the placement of the two side slits, using the washer as a

stencil. Set the washer aside and use a seam ripper or embroidery scissors to cut slits in the interfacing and lining fabric at the marks.

23 Select either the male or female snap with its prongs attached and slip the prongs through the slits from the right side of the lining. Replace the washer over the prongs on the interfacing side and fold the prongs flat toward the outer edge of the snap (**figure 8**). Use flat-nose pliers, if necessary, to grasp and flatten the prongs.

24 Repeat Steps 22–25 to attach the other side of the magnetic snap to the exact center of the Top Band at the front of the lining bag. Before cutting the slits, check the positioning of the snap to ensure that the two sides will meet correctly.

25 With the lining wrong side out and the shell right side out, place the shell inside the lining, aligning the gussets and matching the raw edges. Make sure that the strap is sandwiched between the layers, then pin together along the top edge. Sew slowly and carefully along the entire top edge.

26 Pull the shell through the gap in the lining bag's bottom seam. Tuck in the seam allowances at the opening and slipstitch closed (p. 154). Arrange the lining inside the shell and press the top edge. Topstitch around the top edge of the bag, ¼" (6 mm) from the edge.

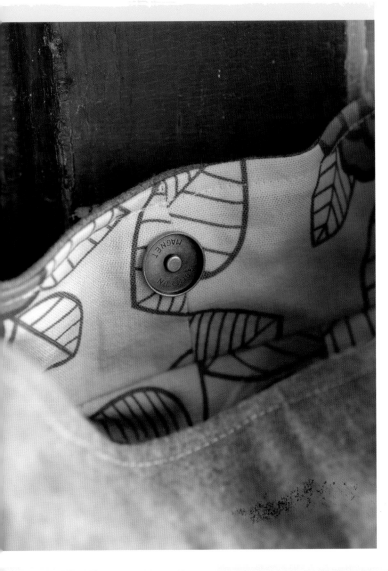

MATERIALS

Main fabrics should be at least 44–45" (112–114.5 cm) wide.

Coordinating sewing thread

Silk thread for appliqués (optional)

Swedish tracing paper (see Resources on p. 158) or other pattern paper (such as butcher paper or newsprint)

WOMEN'S BLOUSE:

2¼ (2¼, 2⅓, 2⅓) yd (2 [2, 2.1, 2.1] m) of lightweight cotton or linen (choose one with a nice drape; Main)

Scrap of floral print cotton for circle appliqués (at least 6½" × 5½" [16.5 × 14 cm])

33" (84 cm) of ½" (1.3 cm)-wide elastic

23" (58.5 cm) of ¼" (6 mm)-wide elastic

CHILD'S BLOUSE:

⅞ yd (80 cm; all sizes) of lightweight cotton or linen fabric (choose one with a nice drape; Main)

Scrap of floral print cotton for circle appliqués (at least 6½" × 5½" [16.5 × 14 cm])

26½" (67.5 cm) of ¼" (6 mm)-wide elastic

TOOLS

Women's or Child's Blossom Blouse pattern (on pattern insert at back of book)

Safety pin

Serger or pinking shears (optional)

Embroidery needle

Circle templates (on pattern insert at back of book) and materials listed under Preparing a Circle on p. 142

MOTHER / DAUGHTER
Blossom Blouse

When I was a Montessori teacher in a one-room schoolhouse in rural Mexico, one of my students showed up in a darling little blouse much like the one you see here. Her grandmother had made it for her in a kitty print, and she wore it with pride. I couldn't help but dream up my own versions in both adult and child sizes (see photo of the child's blouse on p. 84). The bell sleeves and simple shaping make for a flattering drape, while the elastic gathering on the upper arm adds a unique style element.

FINISHED SIZE

WOMEN'S BLOUSE size S (M, L, XL) fits 29½–30½ (31½–32½, 34–36, 38–40)" (75–78 [80–83, 87–92, 97–102 cm]) bust; 19½ (20, 20½, 20¾)" (49.5 [51, 52, 52.5] cm) long from lowered neckline at center back. Blouse shown is size L.

CHILD'S BLOUSE size S (M, L, XL) fits 21–22 (23–24, 25–25½, 26–27)" (53–56 [58–61, 64–65, 66–69] cm) chest; 11¼ (11¾, 12½, 13¾)" (28.5 [30, 31.5, 35] cm) long from lowered neckline at center back. Size S (M, L, XL) corresponds to child's size 2–3 (4–5, 6–6x, 7–8). Blouse shown is size M. The blouse is meant to "grow" with the child, so it would fit more like a tunic on a smaller child and more like a shirt as the child grows.

NOTES

All seam allowances are ½" (1.3 cm) unless otherwise indicated.

See the Pattern Guide on p. 157 for assistance with using patterns and definitions of pattern markings and symbols.

Finish all seam allowances using your preferred method: with the seam allowances together, serge or pink the raw edges or finish with a zigzag stitch (set the stitch length to 1.4 mm and the width to 2 mm; see your sewing machine manual for assistance).

Child's blouse instructions begin on p. 85.

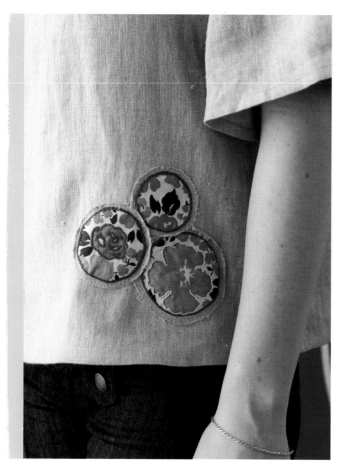

WOMEN'S BLOSSOM BLOUSE

Cut the Fabric

1 Trace the pattern onto Swedish tracing paper or other pattern paper, being sure to transfer all markings and then cut out (or cut the patterns from the pattern insert). Fold the Main fabric in half lengthwise with right sides together and cut the following pieces as directed (refer to the layout diagram on p. 130). Be sure to transfer all pattern markings to the wrong side of the fabric.

> 2 Front/Back on fold (one will be the Front, one will be the Back)
>
> 2 Sleeves on fold

Create the Circle Appliqué

2 Follow the instructions for Preparing a Circle on p. 142 to prepare the templates and then cut and prepare 3 Circles (1 Large, 1 Medium, 1 Small) from the floral print cotton scrap.

3 Hand-appliqué the circles onto a scrap of the same cotton or linen fabric that you are using for the blouse using the standard hand-appliqué stitch (p. 149); make sure you leave at least 1" (2.5 cm) between the circles when appliquéing them to the background fabric.

4 If desired, embellish one or two of the printed flowers (or other shapes) by outlining them with a stem stitch (p. 151) using two strands of embroidery floss. Embroider the outline of each appliquéd circle with a stem stitch in the same manner and then cut out each circle, leaving ¼" (6 mm) of blouse fabric around the edges. Rub the circle edges between your fingers to fray the fabric slightly.

5 With the Blouse Front right side up, arrange the appliquéd circles on top as desired, or see the Assembly diagram at top right for placement. Experiment with overlapping the circles until you are happy with the result.

6 Leaving the bottom-most circle in place, move the other circles aside temporarily. Topstitch (p. 153) the circle in place on the Blouse Front, stitching around the perimeter of the linen circle several times. This will create a rustic look by leaving the raw edges exposed; they will fray slightly with washing. Replace the next circle, overlapping the one already stitched down, and repeat the topstitching, then repeat again to attach the topmost circle.

Assemble the Blouse

7 Place the Front and Back pieces right sides together. Pin and then stitch the side seams. Press the seam allowances toward the back and then finish them using your preferred method (see Notes at left).

8 Cut the ¼" (6 mm) wide elastic in half. *Fold one elastic piece in half and mark the midpoint with a pin, then pin the elastic's midpoint to the center of the sleeve on the guideline transferred from the pattern. Pin the elastic ends to the guideline ends, matching raw edges. Because the elastic is shorter than the sleeve width, it will not lie flat along the sleeve fabric. Set the machine for a standard straight stitch (2.5 mm long; refer to your sewing machine manual for assistance) and anchor the end of the elastic inside the underarm seam allowance by stitching back and forth along the elastic for about ⅜" (1 cm). Stretching the elastic along the guideline, continue to stitch through the center of the elastic to the center pin, then continue to the other end of the guideline and elastic. When you reach the end, anchor the elastic by stitching back and forth within the seam allowance, as before. Repeat from * with the second elastic piece and the other sleeve.

9 Fold one Sleeve in half lengthwise with right sides together. Pin and then sew the underarm seam, matching the elastic ends. Press the seam allowances toward the front and then finish them using your preferred method. Repeat entire step with the second Sleeve.

10 Turn the sleeves right side out and the blouse body wrong side out. *With right sides together, place the sleeve inside the body and match the sleeve armhole raw edges with the raw edges at one raglan armhole of the blouse body. Align the sleeve underarm seam with the body side seam, then pin together around the raglan armhole (for an example of how this is done, see **figure 1** on p. 121). Sew the sleeve and blouse body together along the pinned edge, then trim the seam allowances to about ¼" (6 mm). Press the seam allowances toward the sleeve and finish them using your preferred method. Repeat from * to attach the second sleeve.

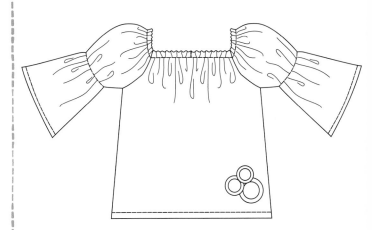

Assembly Diagram

figure 1

Finishing

11 Turn the blouse right side out, then fold over and press ¼" (6 mm) toward the wrong side along the entire neckline. Fold over an additional 1" (2.5 cm) toward the wrong side and press. Topstitch (p. 153) as close to the inner edge of the casing as possible (just shy of 1" [2.5 cm] from the outer neck edge), leaving an opening about 1" (2.5 cm) long at the center back to insert the elastic. This creates an elastic casing with a finished edge on the inside of the blouse.

12 Attach a safety pin to one end of the ½" (1.3 cm)-wide elastic, then insert the safety pin into the casing through the opening and use it to work the elastic through the casing until it reaches all the way around, back to the opening. (To keep the elastic's other end from slipping into the casing, pin it to the blouse before working the elastic into the casing.) Remove the safety pin and distribute the fabric evenly along the elastic, adjusting the length of the elastic for a tighter fit at the neck if desired. Overlap the ends of the elastic by about ½" (1.3 cm) and stitch together securely by stitching back and forth a few times in a zigzag pattern (**figure 1**). Guide the join of the elastic into the casing until it is hidden. Topstitch the opening in the casing closed, matching the previous stitching line.

13 Fold under the hem of one sleeve by ¼" (6 mm), toward the wrong side, and press, then fold over another ¼" (6 mm) and press again. Topstitch as close as possible to the inner edge of the fold (just shy of ¼" [6 mm] from the outer edge of the sleeve opening). Repeat entire step to hem the second sleeve. Repeat again to hem the bottom edge of the blouse, this time folding under ¼" (6 mm) and then ½" (1.3 cm).

Child's Blossom Blouse

CHILD'S BLOSSOM BLOUSE

See **Notes** on p. 82.

Follow Steps 1–8 from the Adult Blossom Blouse on pp. 82 and 83, but in Step 1, fold the selvedges of the Main fabric over, with right sides together, to meet in the middle as shown in the layout diagram on p. 130. Refer to the Assembly diagram at right for assistance with the instructions.

9 Cut 2 pieces of the ¼" (6 mm)-wide elastic, each 4¼" (11 cm) long. Set the stitch length on your sewing machine to 2.5 mm (refer to your sewing machine manual for assistance). With one Sleeve facing wrong side up, anchor the end of one piece of the elastic at one end of the guideline transferred from the pattern, backtacking (p. 152) a few times to secure. Pin the other end of the elastic to the far end of the guideline. Stretch the elastic to span the guideline's entire length as you sew it along the line. Once you reach the end of the line (and your elastic), anchor the elastic once again with several back-tacks (**figure 2**). Repeat the entire step with the second 4¼" (11 cm) elastic piece and the other Sleeve.

Follow the instructions in Steps 9–13 from the Adult Blossom Blouse on pp. 83–84 with the following adjustments.

10 Fold under and press ¼" (6 mm) toward the wrong side along the entire neck edge and then fold over and press an additional ½" (1.3 cm). Topstitch (p. 153) as close as possible to the inner edge of the neck casing (just shy of ½" [1.3 cm] from the outer neck edge), leaving an opening 1" (2.5 cm) long at the center back for inserting the elastic.

11 Use the remaining ¼" (6 mm)-wide elastic to gather the neckline. When you are ready to stitch the ends of the elastic together, overlap the ends by about ½" (1.3 cm) and stitch securely together by sewing back and forth a few times, through both layers (don't forget to backtack to secure; see **figure 1** on p. 84).

12 Fold under and press the hems of both sleeves and the blouse bottom edge toward the wrong side ¼" (6 mm), fold over an additional ¾" (2 cm), and press again. Topstitch each hem as close as possible to the inner edge of the folds (just shy of ¾" [2 cm] from the outer edges).

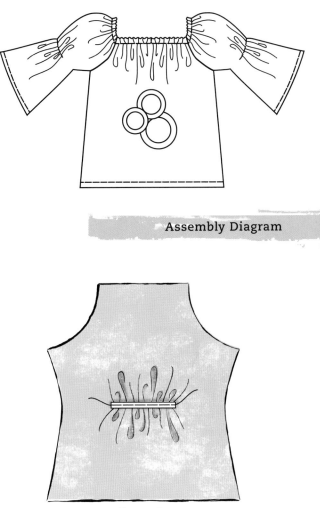

Assembly Diagram

figure 2

MATERIALS

*All fabrics should be at least 45"
(114.5 cm) wide unless otherwise
indicated.*

1 yd (91.5 cm) medium-weight to
heavyweight fabric such as corduroy,
velveteen, or home décor–weight cotton
for Shell (Main)

1¼ yd (1.1 m) cotton print for Lining and
Straps (Contrast)

Scraps of various print fabrics to make
patchwork Pear appliqué (see Step 2 on
p. 88)

4" × 5" (10 × 12.5 cm) scrap of muslin
for appliqué

Brown embroidery floss for Pear stem

⅝ yd (57.5 cm) of ⅜"–½" (1–1.3 cm)-
wide ribbon for side ties (or see the
sidebar on p. 89 to make your own from
the Contrast fabric)

Coordinating sewing thread

Monofilament/invisible thread (optional)

Fray Check (optional)

TOOLS

Pear template (on pattern insert at back
of book) and materials listed under the
Lightweight Fusible Interfacing Method
on p. 138 (you will not need the interfacing because you will be directed to use
the muslin instead)

Buttonhole foot for sewing machine

Blind-hem foot for sewing machine
(optional)

Loop turner or safety pin

FARMER'S
Market Bag

I love how easy it is to whip up this multipurpose bag. The
patchwork pear appliqué is a delectable addition to a bag that
is perfectly suited for gathering yummy produce at your local
farmer's market. The clever design of the bag allows it to easily
expand to hold all of your loot and it would make a perfect gift
for a special friend or neighbor (but you'll want to make one
for yourself as well)!

FINISHED SIZE
28½" (72.5 cm) wide × 14" (35.5 cm) deep
with adjustable straps.

FARMER'S MARKET BAG

Cut the Fabric

1 Cut the following pieces as directed.

From Main fabric

Shell Panel: 32" × 32" (81.5 × 81.5 cm)

Mark four 1¼" (3.2 cm) buttonholes: lay the fabric right side up with the lengthwise grain (p. 152) running up and down. Use a fabric marking pen or tailor's chalk to mark a vertical buttonhole on the fabric at each corner, positioned with the bottom of the buttonhole 4" (10 cm) from the top or bottom edge and 1" (2.5 cm) from the side (**figure 1**).

From Contrast fabric

Lining Panel: 32" × 32" (81.5 × 81.5 cm)

2 Straps: 4" × 42" (10 × 106.5 cm)

Make and Attach Appliqué

2 From the various fabric scraps, cut 5 strips, each measuring 1½" (4.5 cm) wide by 7" (18 cm) long. Pin together two strips, right sides together, along one of the 7" (18 cm) edges. Sew along this edge using a ¼" (6 mm) seam allowance. Continue in the same manner to sew the remaining four strips to form the patchwork panel. Press the seam allowances open.

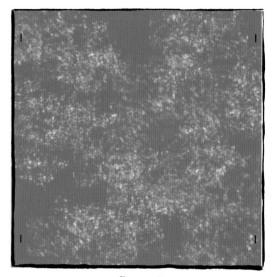

figure 1

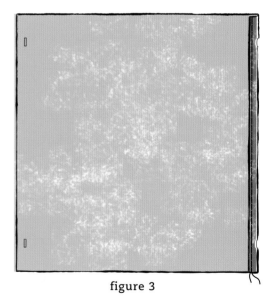

figure 3

figure 2

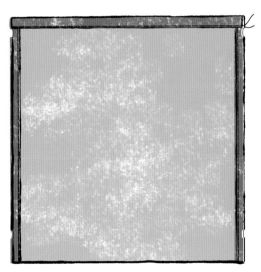

figure 4

MAKING THE SIDE TIES

1 Cut two pieces of Contrast fabric, each 2" × 12" (5 × 30.5 cm).

2 Fold each short edge ¼" (6 mm) toward the wrong side on each tie and press.

3 Fold each tie in half, lengthwise, with wrong sides together, and press. Open the fold and fold each long raw edge in to meet the center fold. Press. Refold the tie along the original center crease and press again.

4 Edgestitch (p. 152) along the pressed edges (the short edges and one long edge) of the ties to finish. Use the prepared ties in place of the ribbon in Step 9.

3 Use the Pear template and the instructions under the Lightweight Fusible Interfacing Method on p 138 to prepare a simple patchwork Pear (cut from the Patchwork Panel just made) for machine appliqué. Substitute muslin for the fusible interfacing called for in the instructions (you won't be able to fuse the pear to the background fabric but pinning will work just fine). Pin the Pear on the Shell Panel, centered from side to side, with the top of the pear 8" (20.5 cm) from one edge, parallel to the buttonhole markings (**figure 2**). If the fabric is directional be sure to place the pear facing the appropriate direction.

4 Hand- or machine-appliqué the pear to the Shell Panel using your preferred method (pp. 146–149; I used a blind hem/invisible stitch [p. 146] and monofilament/invisible thread). Using the brown embroidery floss, embroider a stem at the top of the pear with a chain stitch (p. 150).

Make the Buttonholes and Casings

5 Pin the Shell and Lining Panels wrong sides together, matching the raw edges. Use your machine's buttonhole foot or attachment to sew buttonholes at the markings in each corner through both layers (see your sewing machine manual for more information about the buttonhole function on your machine). Clip the buttonholes open by carefully cutting between the two lines of stitching with embroidery scissors.

6 Fold ½" (1.3 cm) to the lining side along one side edge, parallel to the buttonholes, and press. Fold another ½" (1.3 cm) to the lining side, press, and pin in place. The buttonholes will lie on the very edge of the second fold. Edgestitch (p. 152) along the inner edge of the fold to create a ribbon casing (**figure 3**). Repeat for the opposite edge.

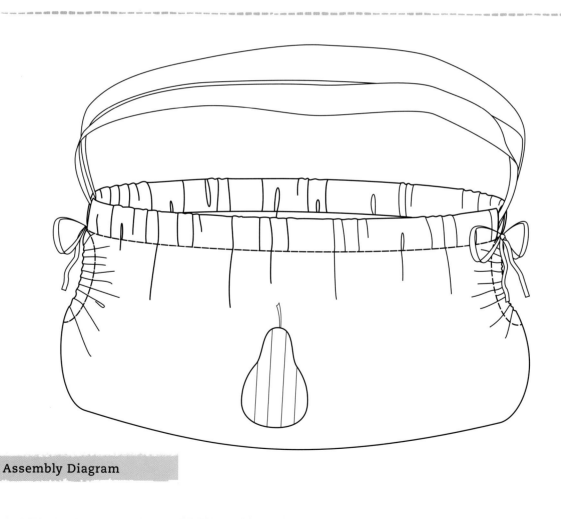

Assembly Diagram

7 Fold ½" (1.3 cm) to the wrong side along one unfinished edge and press. Fold this edge to the wrong side again, lining it up with the top edges of the buttonholes, and press. Pin in place and then edgestitch along the inner edge of the fold (**figure 4**) to create a Strap casing. Repeat for the opposite edge.

Finishing

8 Fold one of the Straps in half lengthwise, with right sides together, pin the long edges together, and sew with a ¼" (6 mm) seam allowance, forming a tube. Use a loop turner or safety pin to turn the tube right side out; to use a safety pin, simply attach it to one layer at one short edge, then work it along the inside of the tube with your fingers until you have turned the tube right side out. Press the Strap flat. Topstitch ¼" (6 mm) from the Strap long edges. Repeat entire step to make the other Strap.

If you plan to create your own ties, follow the instructions in the sidebar on p. 89, then follow Step 9 from *, using the created ties instead of the ribbon.

9 Cut the ribbon in half. *Thread one piece of ribbon through each ribbon casing, entering through one buttonhole and exiting through the opposite one. Use the safety pin to help you as in Step 8. Pull the two ribbon ends, gathering the fabric as tightly as possible, and tie the ribbon ends together in a bow. Use Fray Check on the ends of the ribbon if desired. Repeat entire step to thread the remaining ribbon through the opposite ribbon casing and gather as before (see the assembly diagram at left for assistance).

10 Thread the Straps through the larger strap casings, using the safety pin as in Step 8. Overlap the ends of each Strap by ½" (1.3 cm) and stitch through all layers in a square shape to join the ends securely. Work the Strap around until the join is hidden inside the casing.

sMAll Stitches

PROJECTS FOR BABIES AND CHILDREN

When my husband and I moved to North Carolina after spending three years in rural Mexico (where I taught in a one-room Montessori school), we arrived with a car full of my handmade learning materials and not much else. With my background as an early childhood educator, I've always been passionate about how children learn and experience their surroundings. In the following pages, you will find useful and beautiful projects to enhance your child's experiences, such as the Petit Artiste Smock (p. 119) for painting, drawing, and crafting, and the Little Chef Apron and Hat (p. 125) for shared time in the kitchen. I hope the children in your life will love these creations as much as my students and baby son!

MATERIALS

For the felt, full craft cuts are needed for the book cover and pages, but scraps may suffice for the appliqués.

9 squares of cotton in colors/prints of your choice each 12" × 12" (30.5 × 30.5 cm) for panel backgrounds

Felt in assorted colors (12" × 9" [30.5 × 22.8 cm] craft cuts or ¼ yd [23 cm] pieces) for book cover, pages, and appliqués (shown: aqua, light blue and medium blue for the cover and pages; see templates on pattern insert for the colors shown on individual appliqué pieces [shown: yellow, white, olive green, orange, dark brown, aqua, light green, light blue, medium brown, dark blue, flesh])

Embroidery floss in assorted colors (black is good to have on hand, along with various other colors that match or coordinate with the felts)

Coordinating sewing thread (use assorted colors if you desire)

Template plastic or freezer paper

TOOLS

Baby's First Book templates (on pattern insert at back of book)

10" (25.5 cm) embroidery hoop (I recommend the plastic kind)

Handsewing needle

Embroidery needle

Pinking shears

Fine-tipped permanent marker

BABY'S
First Book

I was so excited when my friend Melissa Crowe, a ridiculously talented felt appliqué artist, agreed to contribute a project to this book. Melissa blogs at checkoutgirlcrafts.blogspot.com and sells her original work at LittlePinkHouse.etsy.com. Her tactile wonder of a baby book couldn't be more perfect. This little heirloom is soft, baby-safe, and a great introduction to simple words when your child reaches that stage in his or her development.

FINISHED SIZE
7" × 5¾" (18 × 15 cm).

BABY'S FIRST BOOK

Cut the Fabric and Prepare the Templates

1 Cut three rectangles from the felt (in your choice of colors), each 12" × 7" (30.5 × 18 cm) for the book cover and page panels. Set aside.

2 Trace each of the templates onto template plastic or freezer paper with a permanent marker and then cut them out with craft scissors, arranging them into piles according to the main label (House, Dog, Cats, Tree, Birds, Boat, Fish, Baby, Cover). Be sure to label each template to make organization easier.

Assemble the House Panel

Refer to the photo below for assistance with the following steps.

3 Select one of the 12" × 12" (30.5 × 30.5 cm) squares as the background for the House panel and secure it in the embroidery hoop.

4 Use the prepared templates to trace and then cut out the House pieces from your assorted felt (one each of the House, Hill, Roof, Dormer, and Dormer Window; two Windows).

5 Position the Hill near the bottom of the background fabric within the perimeter of the embroidery hoop and pin in place. Use a small, even running stitch (p. 151) to

Tips

- Not all felt is created equally. While synthetic felt (including the eco-friendly recycled version) can certainly be used for this project, felt with some wool content will hold up better over time and will give the finished book a richer look and heftier feel. Generally, the higher the wool content, the sturdier the felt. By far the best option for durability and safety, 100% wool felt is available in a certified nontoxic version from some online merchants. Check your local fabric store for inexpensive scrap bags that are perfect for small appliqués!

- I find it easier to use embroidery scissors (rather than sewing scissors) to cut out the smaller appliqués because they allow more control in small spaces and tight curves or corners.

- Be sure to use contrasting colors of felt for the different pieces on each page panel so that the features will stand out, or simply use the colors marked on the templates.

- You can match your thread to each color of felt as you secure the appliqués in place, or simply choose one or a few colors to work with throughout the book.

- Smaller pieces may be easier to attach with a whipstitch (p. 154).

secure the Hill to the background fabric, stitching near the felt's edges.

6 Position the House so its bottom edge sits about halfway up the hill and is centered left to right. Pin and then attach as in Step 5.

7 Position the Roof so it overlaps the top edge of the House slightly. Pin and then attach as in Step 5.

8 Position the Dormer in the center of the roof. Pin in place and attach as in Step 5 using either a running stitch or whipstitch (p. 154) around the edges. Repeat to center the Dormer Window on the Dormer and then attach it.

9 Position the 2 windows on the House, equally spaced between the sides of the house and with their top edges ⅜" (1 cm) below the roof. Pin them in place and then attach as in Step 5 using a running stitch or whipstitch.

10 Using black (or other color, as desired) sewing thread or a single strand of embroidery floss, create window-panes on both Windows and the Dormer Window by backstitching (p. 150; see the photo at bottom left) a vertical and then an intersecting horizontal line on each.

11 Use a fabric marking pen or tailor's chalk to write the word "house" wherever you would like the word to appear, or transfer the word from the template directly onto your fabric according to the instructions on p. 149. When placing the word, keep in mind that the background fabric will be cut down to 5" × 6" (12.5 × 15.2 cm).

12 Using your traced lines as a guide, embroider the word with a backstitch using four to six strands of embroidery floss (shown: black).

13 Remove the fabric from the embroidery hoop, then cut the panel to 5" × 6" (12.5 × 15.2 cm), keeping the appliqués centered and cutting with pinking shears to give the finished panel a fun edge that prevents fraying.

Assemble the Dog Panel

Refer to the photo at left for assistance with the following steps.

14 Repeat Steps 3 and 4 on p. 96, cutting the Dog pieces from the felt (one each of the Hill, Dog Body, Dog Head, Dog Muzzle, and Dog Tail). Cut three small circles (¼" [6 mm] diameter) from the felt for the eyes and nose (shown: black for the nose and white for the eyes).

15 Position the Hill near the bottom of the background fabric within the hoop perimeter. Pin in place and then attach as in Step 5 on p. 96.

TIP: Temporarily place the Dog Body on the hooped fabric to check the Dog Tail position before stitching either piece to the background.

16 Position the Dog Tail along the left side of the hill, as shown in the photo. Pin and attach as before.

17 Position the Dog Body so it is centered side to side with its bottom slightly overlapping the top of the Hill and the Dog Tail. Pin and attach as before.

18 Position the Dog Head so it meets the top of the Dog Body. Pin and attach as before.

19 Position the Dog Muzzle so its bottom edge meets the bottom edge of the head, as shown in the photo. Pin and attach as before.

20 Position the nose near the top of the muzzle and use a tiny whipstitch to secure it in place.

21 Position the eyes on the Dog Head just above the Muzzle and attach with one or two small stitches or a French knot (p. 151) in the center, using black sewing thread or one strand of embroidery floss. These stitches double as the pupils.

22 Repeat Steps 11 and 12 to mark and embroider the word "dog." Then, repeat Step 13 to trim the panel to size.

Assemble the Cats Panel

Refer to the photo at left for assistance with the following steps.

23 Repeat Step 4, cutting the Cat pieces from the felt (one each of Cat Body A, Cat Tail, and Cat Body B; two Cat Heads).

24 Cut a 3" × 4" (7.5 × 10 cm) rectangle of felt (shown: medium blue). Select one of the 12" × 12" (30.5 × 30.5 cm) fabric squares as a background for the Cats panel and position the felt rectangle, oriented horizontally, 3⅜" (8.6 cm) below the top edge of the background and centered side to side; pin in place. Attach the felt to the background fabric with a zigzag stitch (p. 147) around all 4 edges, positioning the stitch to overcast the felt edge.

25 Secure the background fabric in the embroidery hoop with the felt rectangle positioned near the top.

Place the Cat Tail near the left side and just below the felt rectangle, making sure that the curve of the tail does not extend past the side of the felt rectangle, as shown in the photo on p. 96.

26 Position Cat Body A ⅝" (1.6 cm) from the left edge of the felt rectangle, with its bottom left edge overlapping the tail slightly as shown in the photo. Adjust the Tail position if necessary, then pin and attach both Tail and Body A as in Step 5 on p. 96.

27 Position Cat Body B ⅜" (1 cm) from the right side of the felt rectangle, with the bulk of its body lying below the bottom edge of the felt rectangle and overlapping Cat Body A as shown in the photo. Pin and attach as before.

28 Position one Cat Head over each Cat Body so that the Heads meet or slightly overlap the necks. Pin and attach as before.

29 Using black sewing thread or one strand of embroidery floss, stitch a mouth/nose at the center of each Cat Head with two long straight stitches forming an "X". Stitch eyes on each Cat Head with one or two tiny stitches or a single French knot (p. 151) for each eye. Use the same thread to backstitch (p. 150) the outline of a tail on Cat Body B (refer to the photo for assistance with the shape, or transfer the tail line from the Cat Body B template according to the instructions on p. 149).

30 Repeat Steps 11 and 12 on p. 97 to mark and embroider the word "cats" on the felt rectangle or as desired. Repeat Step 13, trimming the panel roughly ⅜" (1 cm) from the felt rectangle at the top and sides, for an overall size of 5" × 6" (12.5 × 15.2 cm).

Assemble the Tree Panel

Refer to the photo at top right for assistance with the following steps.

31 Repeat Steps 3 and 4 on p. 96, cutting the Tree pieces from the felt (one each of the Hill, Tree Trunk, Foliage A, and Foliage B). Position the Hill near the bottom of the background fabric within the hoop perimeter. Pin and attach as in Step 5 on p. 96.

32 Position the Tree Trunk on the Hill, centered from side to side and with the Trunk's bottom edge ⅝" (1.6 cm) above the bottom of the Hill. Pin only the bottom of the Trunk in place. Position Foliage A and B

behind the Tree Trunk branches, making sure the Foliage does not extend beyond the sides of the Hill and that the distance from Hill bottom to Foliage top is no more than 5" (12.7 cm), and pin in place. Move the Trunk aside and attach the Foliage as before. Finish pinning the trunk to the background and attach as before.

33 Repeat Steps 11 and 12 to mark and embroider the word "Tree" on the Hill or as desired. Repeat Step 13.

Assemble the Birds Panel

Refer to the photo at top right for assistance with the following steps.

34 Repeat Step 24 on p. 97, cutting a 4" × 5" (10 × 12.5 cm) rectangle of felt (shown: medium blue) and placing it vertically at the center of the background fabric.

35 Repeat Step 4 on p. 96, cutting the Bird pieces from the felt (one each of Bird Body A, Bird Body B, Wing A, and Wing B). Cut two small triangles for beaks (shown: black).

36 Draw a line 1¾" (4.5 cm) above the felt rectangle's lower edge. Using four to six strands of black or another dark color of embroidery floss, backstitch on the line, creating a wire for the birds to perch on.

37 Position Bird Body A and Bird Body B on the felt rectangle, overlapping the embroidered wire and extending ⅛–¼" (3–6 mm) below it, as shown in the photo. Pin and attach as in Step 5 on p. 96.

38 Place Wing A on Bird Body A and Wing B on Bird Body B, positioning the wings so that they are on the left edge of the bodies and the tips of the wings extend slightly past the left and bottom edges of the bodies, as shown in the photo. Pin and attach as before.

39 Attach beaks to both birds, positioning them near the top of the bodies where the heads would be, using a tiny whipstitch around the edges.

40 Stitch eyes on both birds with a dark color of sewing thread or one strand of embroidery floss, using one or two tiny stitches or a single French knot for each eye.

41 Repeat Steps 11 and 12 on p. 97 to mark and embroider the word "birds" on the felt rectangle. Repeat Step 13.

Assemble the Boat Panel

Refer to the photo above for assistance with the following steps.

42 Repeat Step 24 on p. 97, cutting a 3" × 4" (7.5 × 10 cm) rectangle of felt (shown: light blue) and positioning the felt rectangle, oriented horizontally, 3⅜" (8.6 cm) above the bottom edge and centered side to side on the background fabric. Secure the background fabric in the embroidery hoop.

43 Repeat Step 4 on p. 96, cutting the Boat pieces from the felt (one each of the Boat, Mast, Sail A, Sail B, Porthole, and Flag).

44 Position the Mast, centered left to right, with its lower edge 1⅝" (4.1 cm) above the bottom of the felt rectangle. Pin and attach as in Step 5 on p. 96, but use a whipstitch around the edges instead of a running stitch.

45 Position the Boat, centered left to right, on the felt rectangle so that the top edge overlaps the bottom of the Mast slightly. Pin and attach as in Step 5.

46 Position the Flag at the top of the mast, pointing in either direction, so that the edges are touching as shown and pin in place. Position Sail A and Sail B on either side of the mast, between the Flag and Boat, and pin them in place. Finally, pin the Porthole on the right side of the boat, centered top to bottom. Attach all pieces as before.

47 Repeat Steps 11 and 12 on p. 97 to mark and embroider the word "boat" on the background fabric, making sure the overall length from the bottom of the Boat to the top of the letters is no more than 5" (12.7 cm) and that the letters do not extend beyond the side of the felt rectangle. Repeat Step 13.

Assemble the Fish Panel

Refer to the photo above for assistance with the following steps.

48 Repeat Steps 3 and 4 on p. 96, cutting the Fish pieces from the felt (one each of the Table, Fishbowl, Water, Fish, and Fin). Cut a small circle (¼" [6 mm] diameter) for the fish eye (shown: white).

49 Position the Table, centered left to right, and about ⅝" (1.5 cm) from the bottom of the embroidery hoop. Pin and attach as in Step 5 on p. 96.

50 Position the Fishbowl so it slightly overlaps the top of the Table, keeping the overall appliqué height less than 5" (12.7 cm). Pin and attach as before.

51 Position the Water so that its bottom edge is close to the bottom edge of the Fishbowl, centering the Water from left to right. Pin and attach as before.

52 Position the Fish in the center of the Water. Pin and attach as before.

53 Position the Fin toward the tail of the Fish as shown, then pin and attach as before. Position the eye near the front of the Fish and attach it with a dark color thread or one strand of embroidery floss, using one or two tiny stitches or a French knot at the center of the Eye.

54 Repeat Steps 11 and 12 on p. 97 to mark and embroider the word "fish" on the background fabric. Repeat Step 13.

Assemble the Baby Panel

Refer to the photo at right for assistance with the following steps.

55 Repeat Steps 3 and 4 on p. 96, cutting the Baby pieces from the felt (one each of the Baby Head, Baby Shirt, Baby Pants, and Rug; two Baby Hands).

56 To make the Rug detail, embroider a chain stitch (p. 150) or split stitch (p. 151) around the Rug, ¼" (6 mm) from the edge, using four to six strands of embroidery floss in the color of your choice. Pin the Rug near the bottom of the background fabric within the embroidery hoop perimeter and attach as in Step 5 on p. 96, stitching around the outside of the embroidered detail. If you prefer, position the embroidered Rug, oriented horizontally, 3⅜" (8.6 cm) above the bottom edge of the 12" (30.5 cm) fabric square and machine sew the rug onto the background fabric, using a straight stitch, before hooping.

57 Position the Baby Pants so they overlap the top half of the rug, as shown in the photo. Pin and attach as in Step 5.

58 Position the Baby Shirt so its bottom edge slightly overlaps the top edge of the Pants. Pin and attach as before.

59 Position the Baby Hands, reversing one, so that they meet the edge of the sleeves. Pin and attach as before.

60 Position the Baby Head so the neck slightly overlaps the neck edge of the Baby Shirt, as shown in the photo. Pin and attach as before.

61 Stitch the Baby's eyes with dark sewing thread or one strand of embroidery floss by embroidering a few running stitches in a small star pattern for each eye, or use large French knots. Make a smiling mouth below the eyes with a curved line of backstitches (p. 150).

62 Repeat Steps 11 and 12 on p. 97 to mark and embroider the word "baby" on the background fabric, keeping the overall height less than 5" (12.5 cm). Repeat Step 13 on p. 97.

Assemble the Cover Panel

Refer to the photo at right for assistance with the following steps.

63 Cut a 4" × 5" (10 × 12.5 cm) rectangle of felt (shown: orange) and place it at the center of the hooped background fabric. Pin the rectangle to the background fabric but do not stitch it yet.

64 Repeat Step 4 on p. 96, cutting the Cover pieces from the felt (one each of the Hill, Flower, Flower Center, and Leaf).

65 Position the Hill ¼" (6 mm) from the bottom and left edges of the felt rectangle. Pin and attach as in Step 5 on p. 96.

66 Position the Flower near the top left edge of the felt rectangle, then center the Flower Center on top. Pin and attach as before, stitching the Flower Center through all layers and leaving the edges of the Flower free.

67 Backstitch a stem connecting the Flower to the hill with four to six strands of embroidery floss. Position the Leaf to the left of the embroidered stem and attach it by backstitching along the center through all layers. This will also create the vein of the leaf.

68 Repeat Steps 11 and 12 on p. 97 to mark and embroider "a few of my favorite things" on the right side of the felt rectangle as shown in the photo. Repeat Step 13 on p. 97 with the felt rectangle still pinned to the background fabric.

Finishing

69 Select one of the 12" × 7" (30.5 × 18 cm) felt rectangles cut in Step 1 to use as the cover. Pin the Cover Panel in place on the right side of the felt rectangle, centered from top to bottom, with the pinked edge ¼" (6 mm) from the left side of the felt rectangle. Attach the panel to the large felt rectangle by zigzagging along the edges of the small felt rectangle, through all thicknesses. Set aside.

70 On one of the remaining 12" × 7" (30.5 × 18 cm) felt rectangles, pin one of the Panels in place on the left side as in Step 69, then repeat to pin another Panel in place on the right side. Make sure that there is about 1½" (3.8 cm) between the two Panels in the center of the felt. Repeat entire step to pin two more Panels onto the opposite side of the same felt rectangle, making sure that all Panel tops are facing the same direction. Double check that the Panels are aligned on either side of the felt rectangle because you will be sewing them together

all at once. Machine sew the Panels to the felt with a straight stitch 2.5–3.0 mm long, stitching through all three layers, ¼" (6 mm) from the edge of the Panel lying on top. Go slowly as you stitch the Panels to the felt, checking frequently to be sure the Panel underneath is caught in the stitches, and smooth the fabric often to avoid bunching.

71 Repeat Step 70 to attach the remaining Panels to the remaining felt rectangle.

72 Arrange the pages inside the cover in whatever order you'd like by laying the cover piece right side down, then placing the other two felt rectangles on top, aligning all the edges and making sure that all Panels are facing the same direction (all pictures should be in the same orientation so that you can flip through the finished book). Pin the three felt layers together around the edges. Locate the center of the felt panel and draw two guidelines, one on each side of the centerline and ⁵⁄₁₆" (8 mm) away from the center. Sew a straight machine stitch along each guideline, backtacking (p. 152) at both ends, to join the pages and create the spine (**figure 1**). Fold the book in half widthwise and you are ready to flip through the pages with your little one.

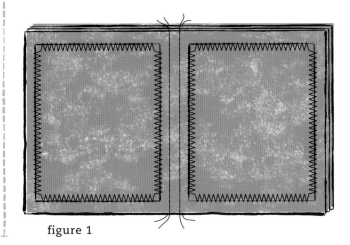

figure 1

MATERIALS

*All fabrics should be at least 45"
(114.5 cm) wide unless otherwise
indicated.*

¾ yd (69 cm) of a heavyweight fabric
such as velveteen, corduroy, or home
décor–weight cotton for Main Panel
(Main)

¾ yd (69 cm) of wool or cotton flannel
for Main Panel Lining (Contrast A)

5 yd (4.6 m) of a heavy cotton fabric
such as home décor–weight or bottom
weight twill for strap (Contrast B)

Scrap of white cotton at least 8 × 8"
(20 × 20 cm) for appliqué

Coordinating sewing thread

TOOLS

Snowflake appliqué template (on pattern
insert at back of book) and materials
listed under the Paper-Backed Fusible
Web method on p. 136

BLANKET
Baby Carrier

Why stay inside when the weather gets chilly? Babies thrive on
a slow, daily walk to take in the sights, sounds, and smells of
the outside world, no matter the season. This carrier is designed to keep those little toes warm as you stroll—the extra
flannel fabric at the bottom can be swaddled around their legs,
a handy feature that other baby carriers omit. For instructions
on how to use the baby carrier see the sidebar on p. 107.

FINISHED SIZE
40½" × 24" (103 × 61 cm) when flat.
Tie is 179" (4.5 m) long.

NOTES

All seam allowances are ½" (1.3 cm) unless otherwise indicated.

Be sure to wash, dry, and press your fabric before sewing; this will prevent further shrinkage from subsequent washings.

You don't have to use the snowflake appliqué template provided—why not make your own? If you're feeling the urge to cut into some paper, go for it! This would also be a great collaborative project with an older child—have the child cut out a snowflake and use that as the appliqué template.

BLANKET BABY CARRIER

Cut the Fabric and Make the Strap

1 Cut the following pieces as directed.

From Main fabric

1 Front Panel: 24" × 36" (61 × 91.5 cm)

From Contrast A

1 Lining Panel: 24" × 36" (61 × 91.5 cm)

From Contrast B

2 Straps: Clear off a lot of floor space so you can completely stretch out the 5 yd (4.6 m) of fabric. Lay out the fabric with the right side facing up. Remove one selvedge by cutting or tearing along the selvedge inner edge. Fold over 7" (18 cm) of the raw edge, creating a double layer down the entire length of the fabric. Cut through the second layer, using the raw edge as a guide, down the entire fabric length (**figure 1**). You now have a 5 yd × 14" (4.6 m × 35.5 cm) strip of fabric. Keep this strip folded in half lengthwise, with right sides together, and pin together down the entire length of the strap and each short edge.

2 Fold the pinned Strap in half widthwise to find the center point and mark at the raw edges with a fabric marking pen or tailor's chalk. Unfold the Strap and mark 12" (30.5 cm) to the left and 12" (30.5 cm) to the right of the center mark on the raw edges. This 24" (61 cm) space is where the Front and Lining Panels will be attached to the Strap.

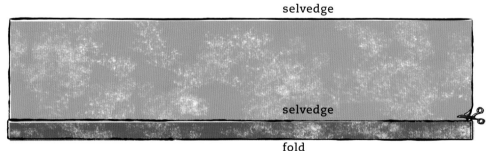

selvedge

selvedge

fold

figure 1

3 Sew along one short edge and the long pinned edge of the Strap, backtacking (p. 152) and trimming the thread when you come to the first mark. Skip over the 24" (61 cm) space and then continue sewing down the length and the remaining short edge. Clip the corners (p. 156) and turn the Strap right side out through the opening. Tuck in the ½" (1.3 cm) seam allowances of the opening and press the entire strap flat. Set aside.

Make and Attach the Snowflake Appliqué

4 Prepare the Snowflake template and then cut and prepare the appliqué according to the instructions under the Paper-Backed Fusible Web method on p. 136, cutting the Snowflake from the white cotton scrap. Use small, sharp embroidery scissors to cut out all the small spaces in the Snowflake.

5 Center the appliqué from side to side on the right side of the Front Panel, 8" (20.5 cm) from one of the short (24" [61 cm]) edges. Follow manufacturer's instructions to fuse the appliqué in place.

6 Use a machine zigzag stitch (p. 147) to appliqué all edges, including the inside edges, of the Snowflake to the Front Panel.

Assemble the Baby Carrier

See the assembly diagram below for assistance.

7 Pin the Front Panel and Lining Panel right sides together, raw edges matched, and then sew together along the bottom and both side edges, leaving the edge closest

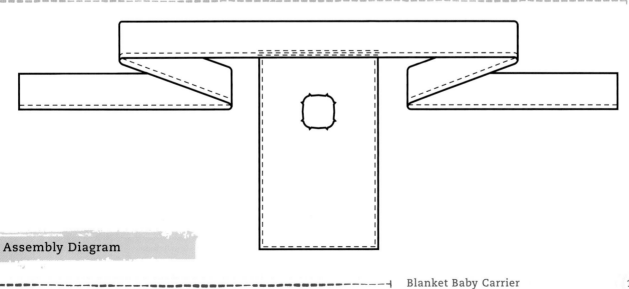

Assembly Diagram

to the Snowflake open. Clip the corners (p. 156), turn right side out, and press flat.

8 Topstitch (p. 153) ¼" (6 mm) from the edge, along the three seamed sides.

9 Insert 1" (2.5 cm) of the Panel's raw edges into the opening of the Strap and pin in place. Edgestitch (p. 152) between the markings on the Strap to close the opening and secure the panel in place. Check frequently to make sure you are catching the Strap layer underneath the Panel in your stitching as well. Topstitch another line of reinforcement stitching ½" (1.3 cm) above the edge-stitched line on the Strap.

10 Beginning at one end of the Strap, topstitch down the entire length of the strap, ¼" (6 mm) from the seamed Strap edge, continuing across the Panel and to the other Strap end. Feel free to use decorative stitches for this final line of topstitching; perhaps a decorative satin stitch (p. 147) would add a nice touch. Be sure to have lots of thread on hand if you choose a satin stitch because the stitches eat up lots of thread.

HOW TO CARRY A BABY ON THE FRONT

These holds are suited for a baby who has good head control.

1 Fold the strap down, right at the seam, toward the right (appliquéd) side. Lay the carrier, right side down, on a sturdy surface such as a bed and place the baby at the top so that his arms are above the fabric (**figure 1**).

2 Fold in the sides of the carrier, over the baby (**figure 2**).

3 Pick up and position the baby on your chest, then pull the straps over your shoulders, crisscross them in the back (pulling to snug the baby carrier against your chest securely and comfortably for both you and baby), and then bring them around your waist, crisscrossing them again right under the baby's bottom (creating a "shelf" for the baby's bottom to rest on). Bring the straps around to the back and tie securely (**figure 3**).

4 Allow the Panel fabric at the bottom to hang free, or tuck it up around the baby's legs for warmth. You can also flip up the strap around the baby's head and tuck in the arms to provide head support and additional warmth (**figure 4**; see also photo on p. 102).

HOW TO CARRY A BABY ON THE BACK

Repeat Steps 1 and 2 above.

5 Pick up the baby and position high on your back, bending over to rest the baby on your back as you pull the straps over your shoulders (**figure 5**).

6 Bring the straps over your arms and under your armpits to the back, crisscrossing them right under the baby's bottom as in Step 3 above. Bring the straps around to the front and tie securely (**figure 6**).

For more information, including an instructional video on how to use the baby carrier, visit my website at sewliberated.com.

Always exercise caution while wearing your baby. Make sure the baby is securely tied in the carrier. Do not use a stove top or bend over from the waist while wearing your baby.

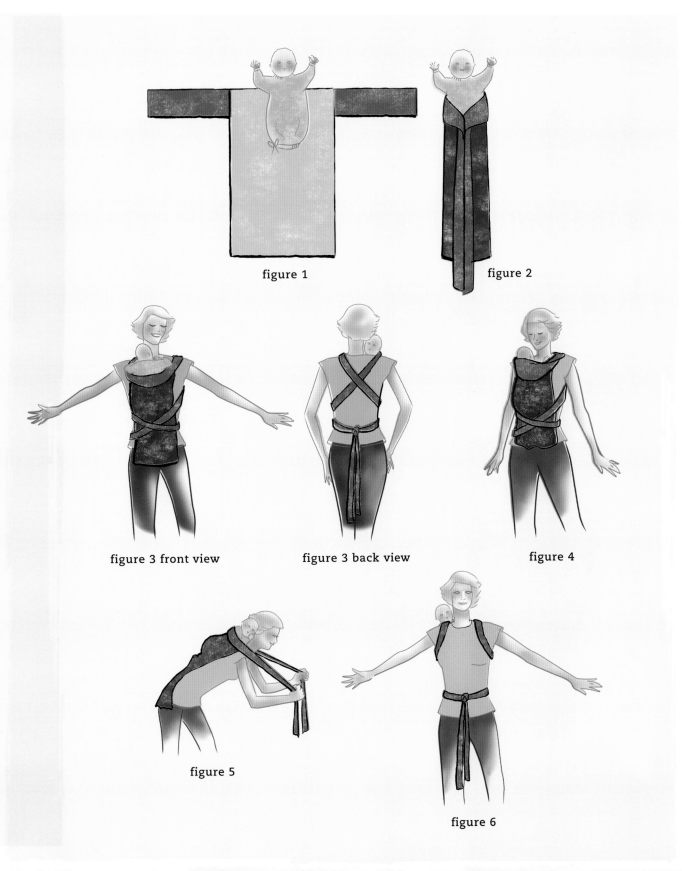

figure 1

figure 2

figure 3 front view

figure 3 back view

figure 4

figure 5

figure 6

MATERIALS

Materials listed are for one bag; all fabrics should be at least 45" (114.5 cm) wide unless otherwise indicated.

½ yd (68.5 cm) of medium-weight wool for shell (Main)

¾ yd (68.5 cm) of medium-weight to heavyweight cotton print for lining (Contrast A)

¼ yd (23 cm) of cotton print for Dog or Ladybug appliqué and coordinating ties (Contrast B)

Coordinating sewing thread

Fray Check

FOR DOG:

6 buttons in various sizes and colors for eye, nose, and four "paws"

1 yd (91.5 cm) of ½" (1.3 cm) wide grosgrain ribbon for legs

Scrap of narrow ribbon for collar (at least 1½" [3.8 cm] long)

FOR LADYBUG:

Scrap of dark colored cotton solid or print for Ladybug Head/Abdomen (see Ladybug template for necessary size)

2 buttons for eyes, each ¾" (2 cm)

2 buttons for antennae tips, each ⅜" (1 cm)

½ yd (46 cm) of ⅛" (3 mm) wide ribbon for antennae

TOOLS

Dog or Ladybug template (on pattern insert at back of book) and materials listed under the Paper-Backed Fusible Web method on p. 136 or your preferred alternate method (pp. 135–145)

Loop turner or safety pin

FUNNY ANIMALS
Children's Tote

Every child needs his or her very own bag—for stowing pajamas and a toothbrush for an overnight trip to Grandma's house or for toting a favorite book to the park. But my goodness, don't we all want a bag that sports such clever decorations? I sure do. I'm sure my son will learn to share his bag with his mama!

FINISHED SIZE

11½" (29 cm) long (not including strap) × 9" (23 cm) wide × 2" (5 cm) deep (front to back). Strap is 23" (58.5 cm) long.

FUNNY ANIMALS CHILDREN'S TOTE

Cut the Fabric

1 Cut the following pieces as directed:

From Main fabric

   2 shell Panels: 13½" × 12" (34.5 × 30.5 cm)

   1 shell Strap: 24" × 3" (61 × 7.5 cm)

From Contrast A fabric

   2 lining Panels: 13½" × 12" (34.5 × 30.5 cm)

   1 lining Strap: 24" × 3" (61 × 7.5 cm)

From Contrast B fabric

   2 Ties: 10" × 2" (25.5 × 5 cm)

Prepare the Bag Front

2 Prepare the Dog or Ladybug template and then cut and prepare the appliqué from the Contrast B fabric (and the dark colored scrap if using the Ladybug), according to the instructions under the Paper-Backed Fusible Web method on p. 136 (or your preferred alternate method [pp. 135–145]). You should have either one Dog Body or one Ladybug Head/Abdomen and two Wings (one left, one right). Then, follow the instructions in the sidebar at right for finishing either the Dog or the Ladybug appliqué.

FINISH THE DOG

1 Remove the paper backing from the Dog, then machine-sew the scrap of ribbon to the Dog's neck using a straight stitch (p. 153) down the middle of the ribbon. Trim the ribbon ends flush with the edge of the dog's body.

2 Cut four slightly varying lengths of grosgrain ribbon for the legs. They can be as short or as long as you want to make them. Center the Dog (right side up) on one of the Main fabric shell Panels (on the right side of the fabric), 5¾" (14.5 cm) below one short Panel edge (this becomes the bag upper edge).

3 Arrange the ribbon legs at the bottom of the Dog's body, slipping ½" (1.3 cm) of each ribbon underneath the appliqué. Fuse the dog body to the bag exterior according to manufacturer's instructions, securing the four legs between the layers. Machine-appliqué along the edge of the Dog using a zigzag stitch (p. 147), leaving the legs dangling.

4 Apply Fray Check to the raw edges of the ribbon legs and let dry. Once the ribbons are dry, sew a button to the end of each. Sew on the eye and nose buttons (see the photo at right).

FINISH THE LADYBUG

1 Remove the paper backing from the Ladybug Head/Abdomen. Center the Head/Abdomen (right side up) on one Main fabric shell Panel (on the right side of the fabric).

2 Cut two pieces of the ⅛" (3 mm)-wide ribbon, each 3" (7.5 cm) long, for the antennae. Arrange one short end of each ribbon so that ¼" (6 mm) of the ribbon is tucked underneath the top edge of the Ladybug Head. Fuse the Head/Abdomen piece in place according to manufacturer's instructions, securing the ends of the ribbon between the layers.

3 Machine-appliqué along the edge of the Head/Abdomen using a zigzag stitch (p. 147). Next, fuse the wings in place over the Ladybug Abdomen (see the photo at bottom right for placement). Machine appliqué around both wings as before.

4 Apply Fray Check to the raw edges of the ribbon antennae. Once the ribbons are dry, secure the ends of the ribbon to the bag fabric, placing them as desired, and tacking them down with a few zigzag stitches. Sew the ⅜" (1 cm) buttons over the ends of the ribbons. Make sure that there is some slack in the ribbon—the antennae should arch away from the bag. Finally, sew on the ¾" (2 cm) eye buttons.

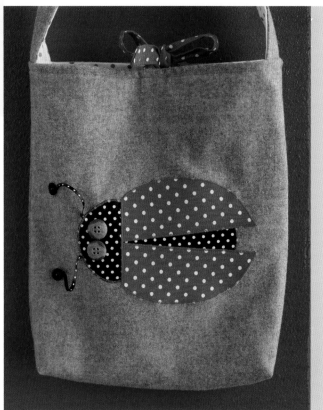

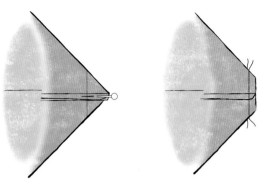

figure 1   figure 2

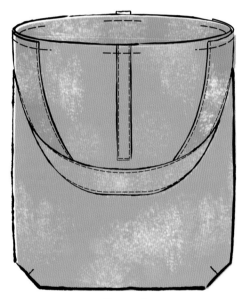

figure 3

Assemble the Lining and Shell

3 Place the Contrast A lining Panels right sides together, aligning all edges, and pin the sides and lower edge. Stitch the pinned edges, beginning at the top of the right side and continuing across the bottom edge for 3½" (9 cm). Backtack (p. 152), lift the presser foot and cut the thread. Move the fabric to position the needle 4" (10 cm) from the backtack along the bottom edge, leaving a gap for turning. Backtack again and continue sewing along the bottom edge and up the left side. Press the seam allowances open.

4 Repeat Step 3 to sew the shell together, placing the front shell Panel (with appliqué) and the remaining shell Panel right sides together. Do not leave a gap for turning.

Square the Bag Corners

5 With the lining still inside out, flatten the bag at one bottom corner so that the side seam lies directly on top of the bottom seam. Pin the layers together close to the corner, then measure 1" (2.5 cm) from the corner along the seam and mark with a fabric marking pen or tailor's chalk. Use a ruler to draw a line across the corner, perpendicular to the seams and passing through the mark just made (**figure 1**).

6 Stitch along the line just drawn. Then, trim the excess fabric from the corner of the bag, leaving a ¼" (6 mm) seam allowance (**figure 2**).

7 Repeat Steps 5 and 6 at the other bottom corner of the lining, then repeat again to square both lower corners of the shell. Once the corners are squared, turn the shell right side out and gently push out the corners.

Create Ties and Strap

8 Press ¼" (6 mm) of one short end of a Tie to the wrong side. Fold the Tie in half lengthwise with right sides together, matching all raw edges. Pin and stitch the long open edge using a ¼" (6 mm) seam allowance, forming a tube. Turn right side out, using a loop turner or safety pin, and press flat; if using a safety pin, simply attach it to one layer at one short edge, then work the safety pin along the inside of the tube until you have turned the tube right side out.

9 Starting at the short raw edge, edgestitch (p. 152) along both long edges and the pressed short edge (with the edges still turned under to the wrong side).

10 Repeat Steps 8 and 9 to make the second Tie. Set both ties aside.

11 Place the two Strap pieces (Main and Contrast A) right sides together, aligning all edges, and pin the long edges together. Sew along the pinned edges, forming a tube.

12 Turn the tube right side out, using a loop turner or safety pin as in Step 8, and press flat. Topstitch ⅜" (1 cm) from each long edge.

Finish the Bag

13 With the shell right side out, pin the Strap raw edges to the unfinished upper edge of the bag, right sides together, centering the Strap ends over the side seams and aligning the shell and Strap raw edges. Be sure the strap remains untwisted. Baste both ends of the strap in place, ¼" (6 mm) from the raw edge (**figure 3**).

14 Fold the bag in half, matching the straps, to find the center front and back points, and mark with pins. Repeat Step 13 to attach one Tie to the center front of the bag and one Tie to the center back of the bag, aligning raw edges and centering each tie over the pinned center locations (see **figure 3**).

15 With the shell right side out and the lining wrong side out, place the shell inside the lining, right sides together. Align the raw edges and side seams and pin together around the top edge, making sure the Strap and Tie ends are sandwiched between the layers. Keep the remainder of the Strap and Ties away from the seamline. Slowly and carefully, sew around the bag's upper edge.

16 Carefully pull the shell through the gap in the lining seam. Turn in the seam allowances at the gap and press. Handstitch the gap closed with a slipstitch (p. 154) or machine stitch if you prefer. Position the lining inside the shell, then press along the top edge for a neat seam. Topstitch around the top of the bag, ⅜" (1 cm) from the edge, using a slightly longer than normal stitch length setting (about 3.0 mm) on your machine.

17 Finally, take a few small, hidden handstitches in each corner of the bag, stitching in the ditch (p. 153) of the seam that squares the lower corner, to fasten the lining to the shell. These tacks keep the lining from shifting and coming out of the bag when little hands are reaching in to pull something out.

MATERIALS

For 2 curtain panels; all fabrics should be at least 45" (114.5 cm) wide.

2⅛ yd (2 m) of cotton print for Top Panels (Main)

1 yd (91.5 cm) of complementary cotton print for Bottom Panels (Contrast A)

3 yd (2.8 m) of home décor–weight cotton for Lining Panels (Contrast B)

4½ yd (4.1 m) of ½" (1.3 cm) wide grosgrain ribbon

Scraps of dark, coordinating cotton or linen for appliqués

Coordinating sewing thread

TOOLS

Squirrel and Acorn templates (on pattern insert at back of book) and materials listed under the Paper-Backed Fusible Web method on p. 136

Yardstick or measuring tape

WOODLAND
Curtains

These cheerful curtains are an homage to a very resourceful mammal—the ubiquitous squirrel. Most children are likely to be familiar with this sprightly creature and would be thrilled to see it gathering acorns right inside their rooms. Open up the curtains, spend a few moments in quiet observation, and you are likely to see a real version skitter across your view and shimmy up a tree.

FINISHED SIZE

Each curtain panel is 35" (89 cm) wide × 50" (127 cm) long (including hanging loops). Window sizes vary, so be sure to measure yours and adjust the dimensions and yardage requirements if necessary.

WOODLAND CURTAINS

Cut the Fabric

1 Cut the following pieces as directed.

From Main fabric

2 Top Panels: 36" × 36" (91.5 × 91.5 cm)

From Contrast A fabric

2 Bottom Panels: 36" × 14" (91.5 × 35.5 cm)

From Contrast B fabric

2 Lining Panels: 36" × 51" (91.5 × 129.5 cm)

Assemble the Curtain Fronts

2 Pin one Top Panel to one Bottom Panel, right sides together, along a 36" (91.5 cm) edge. Sew along this edge and then press the seam allowances toward the Bottom Panel. This creates one curtain front.

3 Cut a 36" (91.5 cm) length of the grosgrain ribbon and position it on the right side of the curtain front, placing it on the Top Panel, adjacent to the seam between the Top and Bottom Panels; one edge of the ribbon will run along the seam but not on top of it. Pin the ribbon in place across the width of the curtain front. Edgestitch (p. 152) the ribbon to the curtain front along each long edge.

4 Repeat Steps 2 and 3 to assemble the other curtain front.

Prepare and Attach the Appliqués

5 Using the provided templates, prepare the Squirrel and Acorn appliqués according to the instructions under the Paper-Backed Fusible Web method on p. 136. Prepare one Squirrel and as many Acorns as you'd like (shown: five acorns).

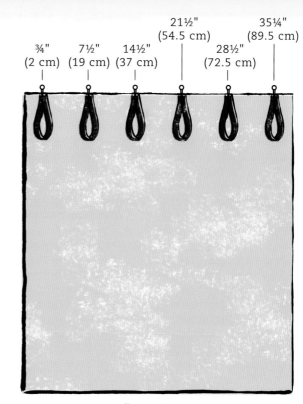

figure 1

6 Following manufacturer's instructions, fuse the appliqués to the Bottom Panel of one curtain front as desired, or see the photo at right for placement. Keep at least ½" (1.3 cm) free of appliqués for seam allowance around the curtain edges. Use a machine zigzag stitch (p. 147) to appliqué around the squirrel and his stash of acorns.

Finishing

7 Cut twelve 7" (18 cm) lengths of grosgrain ribbon for hanging loops. Fold each length of ribbon in half widthwise, matching the short edges to form a loop, and pin. Lay one Lining Panel right side up on the work surface. Using a fabric marking pen or tailor's chalk and yardstick or measuring tape, measure and mark the top (36" [91.5 cm]) edge of the Lining Panel from left to right as follows: ¾" (2 cm), 7½" (19 cm), 14½" (37 cm), 21½" (54.5 cm), 28½" (72.5 cm), and 35¼" (89.5 cm). Pin the raw edges of one loop at each mark, matching the raw edges of the ribbon loops and Lining Panel, with the ribbon loops lying on the Lining Panel (**figure 1**). Repeat entire step to add hanging loops to the remaining Lining Panel.

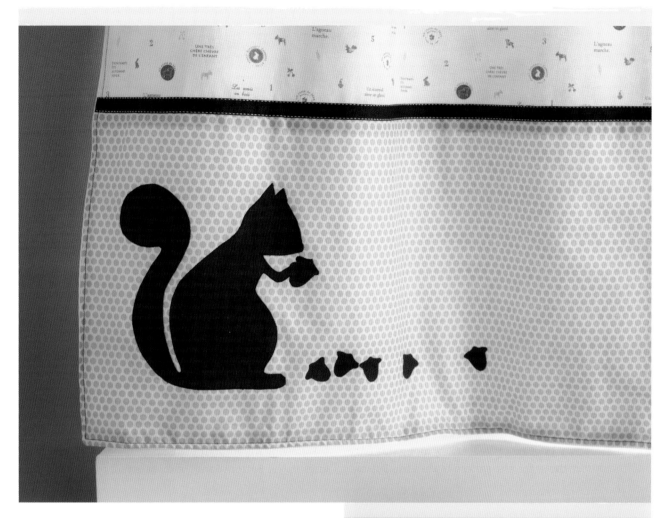

8 Pin one curtain front to each Lining Panel, right sides together, raw edges matched, and with the hanging loops sandwiched between layers along the top edges of the curtain front and lining. Sew along all four edges of each curtain, leaving a 5" (12.5 cm) opening along one side of each curtain for turning.

9 Turn each curtain right side out. Tuck in the seam allowances at the openings and press the curtains flat. Topstitch (p. 153) ¼" (6 mm) from the edge around all four edges of each curtain.

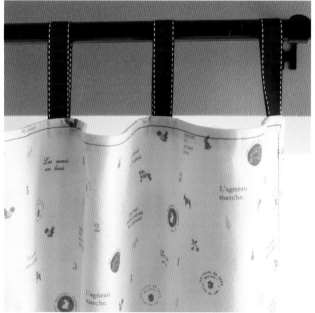

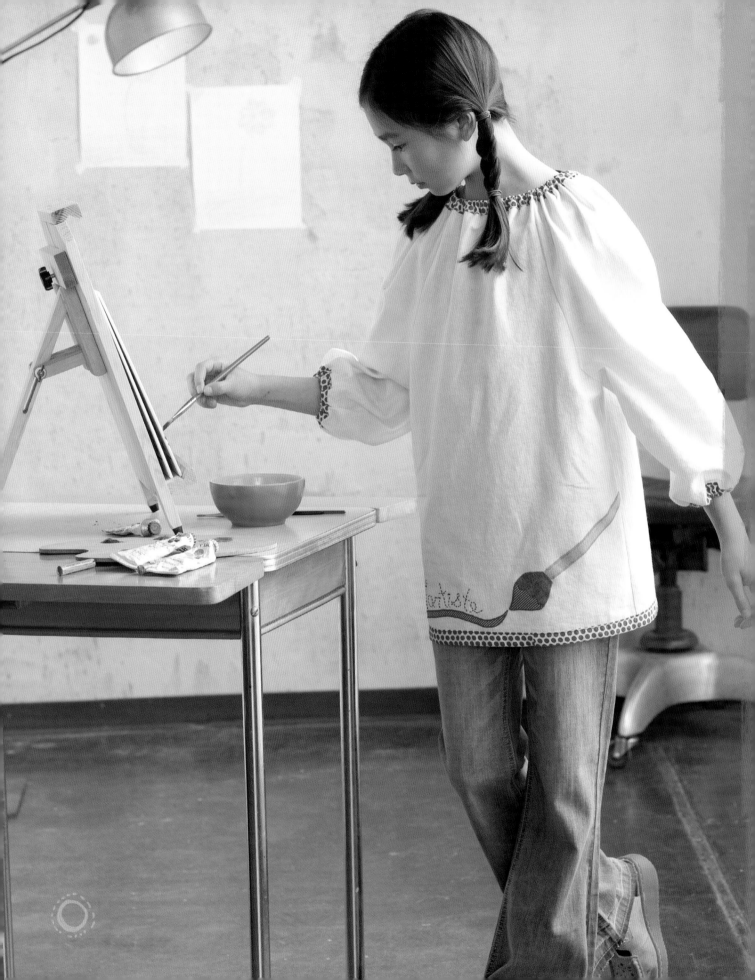

MATERIALS

*All fabrics should be at least 45"
(114.5 cm) wide unless otherwise
indicated.*

1¼ yd (1.1 m) of cotton for smock
(Main)

½ yd (46 cm) of contrasting cotton print
for casings/bindings (Contrast)

3 scraps of various fabrics for appliqués
(see templates on pattern insert at back
of book for necessary sizes)

12" (30.5 cm) of ¼" (6 mm)-wide elastic
for sleeves

19½" (49.5 cm) of ½" (1.3 cm) wide
elastic for neck

Matching or coordinating sewing threads
for Main fabric, Contrast, and appliqués

Coordinating embroidery floss (shown:
red)

TOOLS

Petit Artiste Smock pattern (on pattern
insert at back of book)

Swedish tracing paper (see Resources
on p. 158) or other pattern paper (such
as butcher paper or newsprint)

Petit Artiste templates (on pattern insert)
and materials listed under the Paper-
Backed Fusible Web method on p. 136

L'artiste embroidery template (on pattern
insert) and materials listed on p. 149 for
transferring the design

Serger or pinking shears (optional)

Safety pin

PETIT ARTISTE
Smock

This child's art smock will make your little Picasso feel special
and keep him or her clean! Originally designed for use in my
Montessori classroom of 2½- to 6-year-olds, this smock features an easy on/off design so that a child can confidently and
independently partake in artistic endeavors. Demonstrate for
the child how to pull the elastic neckband over his head with
the open back of the smock facing him. With the loose design
and open back, this smock will probably fit your child for several years and will make a perfect hand-me-down to a younger
sibling, cousin, or friend.

FINISHED SIZE

One size fits all; sizes 4–6X. Smock is
23" (58.5 cm) long from shoulder to hem
and 16" wide (40.5 cm) at underarm,
with the back left open for adjustable
fit and ease of putting on and taking
off. Wrist openings are 5" (12.5 cm) in
circumference with elastic that can
be stretched up to 17½" (44.5 cm) for a
comfortable fit. Elasticized neck opening is 19" (48 cm) in circumference.

NOTES

All seam allowances are ½" (1.3 cm) unless otherwise indicated.

Be sure to wash, dry, and press your fabric before sewing to prevent further shrinkage from subsequent washings.

Since the smock will probably get its fair share of washing, be sure to finish all seam allowances using your preferred method: with the seam allowances together, pink the raw edges or finish with a serger or zigzag stitch (set the stitch length to 1.4 mm and the stitch width to 2.0 mm; see your sewing machine manual for assistance).

See the Pattern Guide on p. 157 for assistance with using patterns.

PETIT ARTISTE SMOCK

1 Trace the Petit Artiste Front/Back and Sleeve pattern pieces onto Swedish tracing paper or other pattern paper, transferring all pattern markings, and cut out.

Cut the Fabric

2 Cut the following pieces as directed and using the indicated pattern pieces; refer to the layout diagram on p. 133 for assistance.

From Main fabric

One Front/Back on fold (mark as front)

Two Sleeves on fold

Two Front/Backs not on fold (mark as backs)

From Contrast fabric

Five strips: 3⅛" (7.9 cm) wide and cut across the entire fabric width for the binding/casings. Remove the selvedges from each strip.

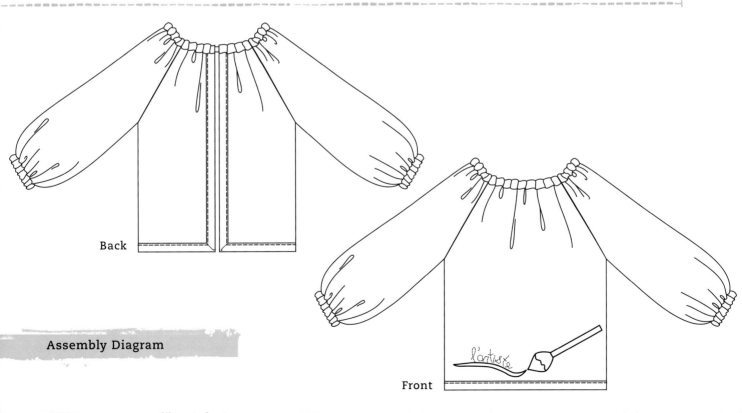

Back

Assembly Diagram

Front

l'artiste

Assemble the Smock

3 Place the front and both back pieces right sides together, matching the side edges. Pin together and sew the side seams. Finish all seam allowances using your preferred method (see Notes at left). Press the seam allowances toward the back.

4 Fold one sleeve in half lengthwise with right sides together, matching the raw edges for the underarm seam. Pin and stitch the underarm seam. Finish the seam allowances using your preferred method, and then press them toward the front. Repeat entire step with the second sleeve. Turn both sleeves right side out.

5 With the smock body still inside out, place one sleeve inside the smock body and match the sleeve armhole edges with the raw edges of one front/back raglan (p. 153) armhole (right sides will be together). Align the underarm seam of the sleeve with the side seam of the smock body, then pin together around the raglan armhole (**figure 1**). Sew along the pinned edge, finish the seam allowances using your preferred method, and then press seam allowances toward the sleeve. Repeat entire step to attach the second sleeve.

Make and Attach Binding

6 Follow the instructions under Double-Fold Binding on p. 154 to create the binding with the five Contrast strips cut in Step 2.

7 Follow the instructions under Attaching Binding with Mitered Corners on p. 155 to bind the smock's bottom and center back edges.

Attach Casings and Insert Elastic

Note: Figures 2 and 3 appear on p. 123.

8 Using the remaining binding from Step 6, create casings on both sleeve openings. Begin by opening one short end of the binding and pressing ½" (1.3 cm) to the wrong side. Refold the binding along the center crease and press again.

9 Slide the folded binding strip over the sleeve opening raw edge, with the pressed end at the underarm seam, so that ¼" (6 mm) of the sleeve opening raw edge is inside the folded binding. Pin the binding around the entire sleeve raw edge in this manner. Trim the excess binding ½" (1.3 cm) beyond the underarm seam after

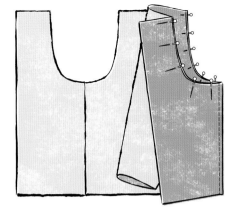

figure 1

you have come all the way around. Unfold the binding slightly and turn the extra ½" (1.3 cm) toward the wrong side as before and finger press (p. 152) the fold. Then, pin the folded-under end of the binding to the sleeve edge, so the two pressed binding ends meet at the underarm seam.

10 Topstitch (p. 153) the casing to the sleeve, sewing ⅛" (3 mm) or less from the binding fold (**figure 2**). Check frequently to be sure the stitches are catching the fold of the binding inside the sleeve as well.

11 Repeat Steps 8–10 for the second sleeve.

12 Using the remaining binding, create a casing at the neck edge. Follow the instructions given for the sleeve casings in Steps 8–10, but position the binding strip's pressed short ends at the neckline's center back edges.

13 Cut the ¼" (6 mm)-wide elastic in half. *Attach a safety pin to one piece of ¼" (6 mm)-wide elastic and guide it through the sleeve casing, beginning at the underarm seam opening and working the safety pin along the inside of the casing until it comes back around to the other opening. Pull both ends of the elastic out through the openings just enough to overlap them by about ½" (1.3 cm). Stitch the ends of the elastic securely together by sewing back and forth through both layers as shown in **figure 3**. Stretch the cuff so the elastic slides back into the casing. Handstitch the pressed casing ends together with a slipstitch (p. 154) to close the opening at the underarm seam.

Repeat entire step from * for the second sleeve, using the second half of the ¼" (6 mm) wide elastic.

14 Now, thread the 19½" (49.5 cm) length of ½" (1.3 cm) wide elastic through the neck casing, using a safety pin in the same manner as in Step 13. Thread the elastic through one of the open ends of the casing, exiting from the opposite side. Pull both ends of the elastic out enough to overlap them by about 1" (2.5 cm). Stitch the ends of the elastic securely together by sewing back and forth through both layers as shown in **figure 3**. Work this seamed area of elastic around to the front of the casing so that it doesn't show in the back. You will be able to see a bit of elastic at the center back opening. This makes a perfect little tab of elastic to hang the smock from a hook next to the art area for easy storage!

Add Appliqué and Embroidery

15 Prepare the templates and then cut and prepare the appliqués (1 Paintbrush Handle, 1 Paintbrush, 1 Paintbrush Tip, and 1 Paint) according to the instructions under the Paper-Backed Fusible Web method on p. 136, using the fabric scraps.

16 Arrange the appliqué pieces as desired on the front of the smock or refer to the assembly diagram on p. 120 for placement. Once you are happy with the placement, pin only the Paintbrush Handle in place, then attach it with a zigzag stitch (p. 147) around the edges. Next, place the Paintbrush piece so that it is touching the end of the Handle, then pin and attach as before. Repeat to attach the Paintbrush Tip, positioning it so that it overlaps the bottom edge of the Paintbrush piece slightly.

Finally, pin the Paint piece near the Paintbrush Tip and attach as before.

17 Prepare and then transfer the "l'artiste" embroidery template to its location just above the Paint, according to the instructions on p. 149. Alternatively, use a fabric marking pen or tailor's chalk to draw in the word free-hand.

NOTE: Do not use a permanent pen to transfer the embroidery template, as the embroidery stitches will allow the pen marks to show through.

18 Embroider over the drawn or transferred lines using a running stitch (p. 151; see the photo below). After embroidering, remove the pen marks with water or as directed by the manufacturer. Now your little artist is ready to create a masterpiece!

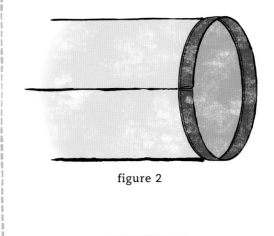

figure 2

figure 3

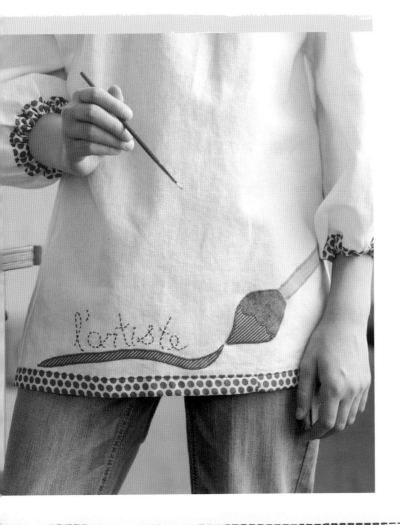

MATERIALS

*All fabrics should be at least 44–45"
(112–106.5 cm) wide unless otherwise
indicated.*

1¾ yd (1.6 m; all sizes) of cotton or
cotton/linen blend print for Apron body,
Hat Top, and appliqués (Main)

½ yd (46 cm) of solid cotton or linen for
Apron Belts and Pocket and Hat Band
(Contrast)

Contrasting sewing thread

LITTLE CHEF APRON:

6" (15 cm) of ¾" (2 cm) wide Velcro for
belt closure

LITTLE CHEF HAT:

1¼ yd (1.1 m) of lightweight fusible
interfacing (at least 22" [56 cm] wide)

5" (12.5 cm) of ¾" (2 cm)-wide Velcro
for hat closure

8" (20.5 cm) of coordinating ¼" (6 mm)
to ½" (1.3 cm) wide double fold bias
tape (or make your own from the leftover
Main fabric [see p. 154])

TOOLS

Little Chef Apron and/or Little Chef Hat
Patterns (on pattern insert at back of
book)

Swedish tracing paper (see Resources
on p. 158) or other pattern paper (such
as butcher paper or newsprint)

Serger (optional)

Materials listed under the Paper-Backed
Fusible Web method on p. 136 for the
simple appliqué (will be cut from the
Main print fabric)

LITTLE CHEF
Apron and Hat

Get out the flour! Get out the bowls! There is, perhaps, no
greater fun than cooking up a storm with a young child. This
chef's apron and hat set will make your little cook feel like the
real deal, not to mention providing some protection for the
cook's clothes. The hat features an easy-on, adjustable Velcro
closure and the apron has a special, wrap-around waistband
that attaches in the front so that the child can be independent
in putting it on and taking it off. Hang the apron and hat from a
low hook in the kitchen so that they are always ready for use!

FINISHED SIZE

APRON fits 25–30 (33–38)" (63.5–76 [84–
96.5] cm) waist circumference; sizes:
2–5 (6–8).

CHEF HAT is one size fits all, with a
20–22" (51–56 cm) head circumference
(Velcro closure is adjustable).

NOTES

All seam allowances are ⅜" (1 cm) unless otherwise indicated.

Remember to wash, dry, and press all fabric before you start sewing to prevent further shrinkage from subsequent washings.

See the Pattern Guide on p. 157 for assistance with using patterns.

If you plan to make both the Apron and the Hat, cut the Main fabric pieces all at once to ensure that you use the fabric to the best advantage. See the layout diagram on p. 132.

LITTLE CHEF APRON

1 Trace all pattern pieces onto Swedish tracing paper or other pattern paper, transferring all pattern markings, and cut out.

Cut the Fabric

2 Cut the following pieces as directed (refer to the layout diagram on p. 132 for assistance). Be sure to transfer all pattern markings to the wrong side of the fabric.

From Main fabric

4 Apron Body: 2 for the shell, 2 for the lining

From Contrast fabric

4 Belt

2 Pocket

Prepare the Pocket and Belt

3 Follow the instructions under the Paper-Backed Fusible Web method on p. 136 to prepare and cut a motif from the Main fabric to use as the appliqué; apply the fusible web to the wrong side of the fabric, directly underneath the motif you would like to use before cutting. Make sure that the motif is no more than 2¾" (7 cm) tall.

my favorite BREAD

Our family's favorite bread recipe is perfect for making alongside a child. When I was teaching in a classroom of three- to six-year-olds, the oldest of the bunch had this recipe memorized and could make their own bread without any help. How wonderfully uplifting it was to have the aroma of fresh-baked bread wafting through the classroom!

Ingredients:

2 cups warm water	1 tsp. salt
2 cups whole wheat flour	⅓ cup honey
5 cups all-purpose flour	⅓ cup vegetable oil
1 tbsp. yeast	

Directions:

Dissolve the yeast in the warm water. Add the honey and stir. Meanwhile, in a large bowl, mix together the salt, whole wheat flour, and two cups of all-purpose flour. Pour in the yeast mixture and add the oil. Work in the remaining all-purpose flour gradually. Turn dough out onto a lightly floured surface and knead for 10–15 minutes. When it is smooth and elastic in consistency, place in an oiled bowl. Turn several times to coat with oil and cover with a damp cloth. Let rise in a warm place until the dough has doubled in size—about 1 hour. Punch down the dough and shape on a greased cookie sheet, or place in two 9" × 5" (23 × 12.5 cm) well-greased loaf pans. Cover with a damp cloth and let rise for another 20–30 minutes. Bake at 375° F for 25–30 minutes.

4 Place one Pocket piece in front of you, right side up. Remove the paper backing from the appliqué and follow manufacturer's instructions to fuse it, centered, onto the Pocket. Use a small zigzag stitch (p. 147; about 1.5 mm wide and 1 mm long, see your sewing machine manual for assistance with the settings) to secure the appliqué to the pocket.

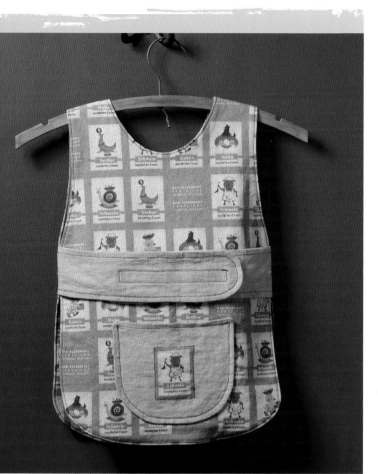

half of the Velcro to the right side of the remaining Belt (the Velcro is positioned so that the two pieces fasten to close the belt; see the assembly diagram on p. 128).

Prepare Apron Front and Back

8 With the right side of one Apron Body facing up, pin the Pocket in place, centered left to right and with the Pocket lower edge 1½" (3.8 cm) above the bottom edge of the Apron Body (see diagram on p. 128). Topstitch ¼" (6 mm) from the curved pocket edges (sides and bottom), leaving the pocket top open. This is now the apron front; set aside.

9 With the right side of another Apron Body facing up, fasten the Belts to each other with the Velcro and place them on the Apron Body with the Belt's lower edge 10" (25.5 cm) above the bottom edge of the Apron Body, matching raw edges at the side seams. Pin the Belts in place. Machine-baste (p. 152) each belt end in place, about ¼" (6 mm) from the raw edge. This is now the apron back.

Assemble the Apron

10 With the Belts still fastened, pin another of the remaining Apron Body pieces to the apron back, right sides together. *Leaving the shoulders unseamed, sew along the sides, bottom, and neckline apron edges, leaving a 3" (7.5 cm) gap along the straight portion of one side for turning. Clip the curves and corners and turn right side out. Tuck in the seam allowances along the 3" (7.5 cm) opening and press flat. Edgestitch around the entire edge of the apron (with the exception of the shoulder seams, which will be finished later), closing the gap along the way.

11 Pin the last remaining Apron Body piece to the apron front created in Step 8, right sides together. Repeat Step 10 from * to complete the apron front.

12 Pin the apron back to the apron front at the shoulder seams, right sides together.

NOTE: The right side of the apron front is the pocket side. The right side of the apron back depends on whether the child is right-handed or left-handed: the belt should open from the side of the child's dominant hand. In other words, a right-handed child should be able to open the belt with his right hand, so the portion of the belt that lies on top should be on the wearer's right.

5 Place the two Pocket pieces right sides together and pin. Sew together around the entire perimeter, leaving a 2" (5 cm) gap for turning along the straight upper edge. Clip the seam allowances along the curves (p. 156) and at the corners (p. 156). Turn the pocket right side out and tuck in the seam allowances at the gap; press flat. Topstitch (p. 153) along the top edge of the pocket, about ¼" (6 mm) from the edge, closing the opening.

6 Place two of the Belt pieces right sides together and pin. Sew around the edges, leaving the short, straight edge open for turning. Clip the seam allowances around the curve, then turn right side out and press flat. Topstitch around the entire finished seam, ¼" (6 mm) from the edge. Repeat entire step to make the second Belt.

7 Lay one half of the 6" (15 cm) piece of Velcro on the wrong side of one Belt, centered top to bottom and with one end ¾" (2 cm) from the curved edge of the Belt; pin in place. Edgestitch (p. 152) around the perimeter of the Velcro to secure. Repeat entire step to attach the other

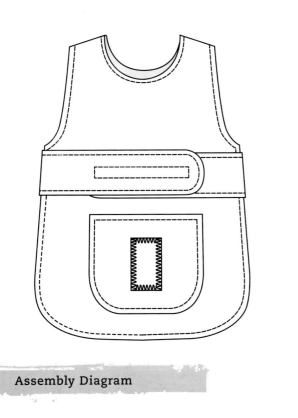

Assembly Diagram

13 If you have a serger, use an overlock stitch (p. 153) to sew the two shoulder seams; press the seam allowances toward the back. If you do not own a serger, sew the shoulder seams with a conventional machine and finish the seam allowances with a zigzag stitch or by pinking them before pressing the seam allowances toward the back. If desired, tack the corners of the seam allowances down (to the apron lining) with a few handstitches to keep them out of sight.

CHEF'S HAT

See **Notes** on p. 126.

14 Trace all pattern pieces onto Swedish tracing paper or other pattern paper, being sure to transfer all pattern markings, and cut out.

Cut the Fabric

15 Cut the following pieces as indicated (refer to the layout diagram on p. 132 for assistance). Be sure to transfer all pattern markings to the wrong side of the fabric.

From Main fabric

1 Hat Top

From Contrast

1 rectangle: 8" × 25" (20.5 × 63.5 cm) for Hat Band

From Interfacing

1 Hat Top

1 rectangle: 8" × 25" (20.5 × 63.5 cm) for Hat Band

NOTE: It will be necessary to piece the interfacing Hat Band. Cut two strips 8" (20.5 cm) wide, across the entire interfacing width. When applying the interfacing to the Hat Band in Step 2, overlap the short ends approximately ¼" (6 mm). Then, trim the excess interfacing at one end of the Hat Band.

Prepare the Hat Top and Band

16 Following manufacturer's instructions, fuse the interfacing pieces to the wrong sides of the Hat Top and Hat Band.

17 Fold the Hat Band in half lengthwise, right sides together. It should now measure 4" × 25" (10 × 63.5 cm). Pin and stitch the short ends. Trim the corners, turn right side out, and press flat.

18 Follow the instructions under the Paper-Backed Fusible Web method on p. 136 to prepare and cut three motifs from the Main fabric to use as the appliqués; apply the fusible web to the wrong side of the fabric, directly underneath the motifs you would like to use, before cutting. Make sure that the motifs are no more than 2¾" (7 cm) tall. Following manufacturer's instructions, fuse the appliqués to the center of the Hat Band so that the motifs are centered (top to bottom) and the bottoms of the motifs face the folded edge of the Hat Band, which is the bottom edge of the hat.

19 Once the motifs are fused, carefully open the Hat Band in order to stitch down the appliqués with a zigzag stitch (your zigzag stitch [p. 147] should only go through one layer of the Hat Band, not both). Set aside the Hat Band for now.

20 If you are using ready-made bias tape, skip to Step 21. If you are making your own bias tape, use the leftover Main fabric and follow the instructions under Double-Fold Bias Binding on p. 154.

21 Cut a 3½" (9 cm) slit in the Hat Top, following the marking on the pattern (**figure 1**). Spread the slit wide apart so it forms a straight line and encase the raw edges with the bias tape by snugging the raw edge up into the bias tape's center crease. Pin the bias tape in place and begin edgestitching the bias tape a scant ⅛" (3 mm) from its inner edge (see the assembly diagram at right). Go slowly as you near the center of the slit, pulling the fabric taut and being careful not to stitch any tucks or gathers; check often to be sure that the bottom edge of the binding is also being caught in the stitches. Cut off any extra binding so that it is flush with the edge of the Hat Top.

Assemble the Hat

22 Sew two rows of machine-basting stitches around the edge of the Hat Top, approximately ¼" (6 mm) and ⅜" (1 cm) from the raw edge, starting and ending each row at the slit. Don't backtack (p. 152) at either end of the stitching, and leave thread tails (at least 3" [7.5 cm] long) at each end.

23 Fold the Hat Band in half widthwise, so that the short edges meet, to find the center point, and mark the center on the raw edges. Pin the Hat Band to the Hat Top, right sides together; be sure to align the raw edges, matching the center marks and matching the Band's short ends to the slit edges on the Hat Top. Pull gently on the bobbin threads of the machine-basting stitches on the Hat Top to gather the fabric from one side of the slit toward the center notch. Distribute the gathers evenly along the thread by sliding the fabric along the tightened thread with your fingers. Gather the other side of the Hat Top toward the center, by pulling on the bobbin threads from the opposite side.

24 Continue to gather the Hat Top as needed until it fits perfectly with the Hat Band and then continue to pin the Hat Top to the Band.

25 Sew the Hat Top and Hat Band together around the pinned edge. Flip the Band down and then press the seam allowances toward the Band. Topstitch along the top of the Band (where it meets the Hat Top), ¼" (6 mm) from the edge (see assembly diagram at right).

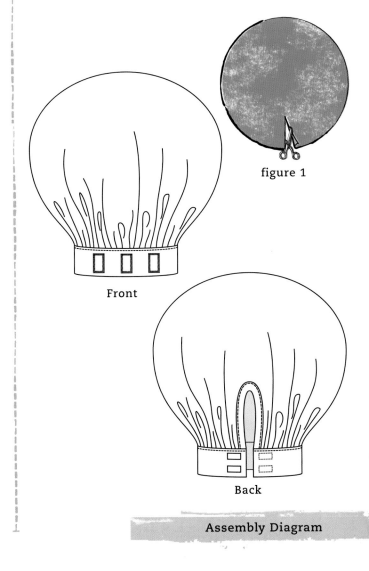

figure 1

Front

Back

Assembly Diagram

Finishing

26 Cut the 5" (12.5 cm) of Velcro in half. *With the back of the hat (with the slit) facing you, pin and sew the two rough (hook) sections of Velcro to the right side of the left band end as shown on the Back assembly diagram, edgestitching around the perimeter of the Velcro. Position the bottom piece of Velcro about ½" (1.3 cm) from the band end and ½" (1.3 cm) above the bottom of the Hat Band. Align the second piece of Velcro ¾–1" (2–2.5 cm) above the first piece.

27 Repeat Step 26 from * to attach the two soft (loop) sections of the Velcro to the wrong side of the right end of the Hat Band, making sure that the Velcro sections on both ends will meet to fasten the Hat Band.

PATTERN LAYOUT DIAGRAMS

Women's Blossom Blouse
44"–45" (112–114.5 cm) fabric
S–M 2¼ yd (2.05 m)
L–XL 2⅓ yd (2.13 m)

Child's Blossom Blouse
44"–45" (112–114.5 cm) fabric
All sizes ⅞ yd (0.8 m)

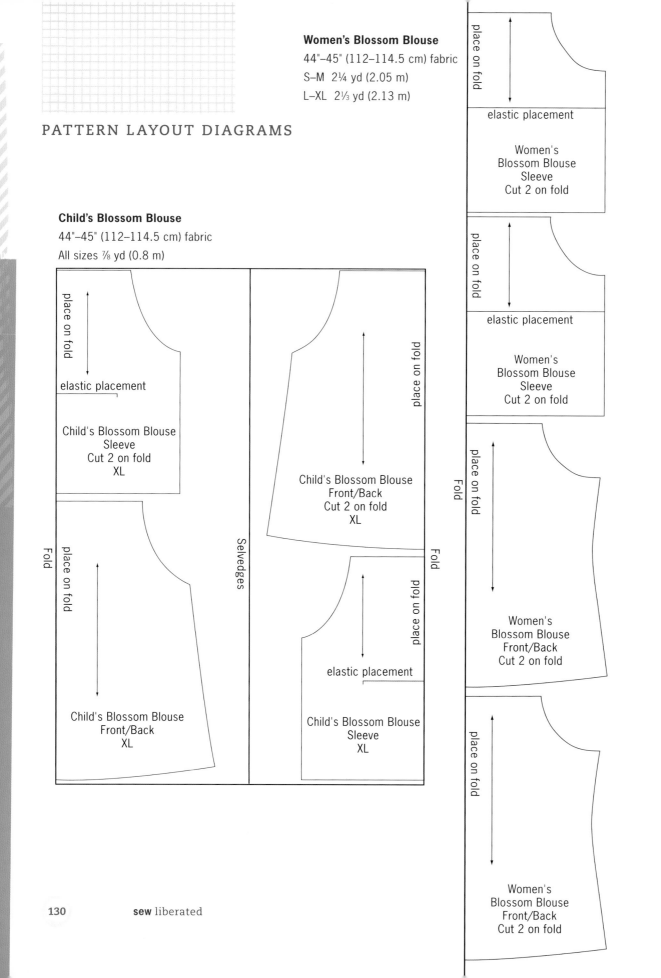

place on fold

elastic placement

Women's
Blossom Blouse
Sleeve
Cut 2 on fold

place on fold

elastic placement

Women's
Blossom Blouse
Sleeve
Cut 2 on fold

place on fold

Fold

Women's
Blossom Blouse
Front/Back
Cut 2 on fold

place on fold

Women's
Blossom Blouse
Front/Back
Cut 2 on fold

Selvedge

place on fold

elastic placement

Child's Blossom Blouse
Sleeve
Cut 2 on fold
XL

place on fold

Child's Blossom Blouse
Front/Back
XL

Fold

place on fold

Child's Blossom Blouse
Front/Back
Cut 2 on fold
XL

place on fold

elastic placement

Child's Blossom Blouse
Sleeve
XL

Fold

Selvedges

Selvedges

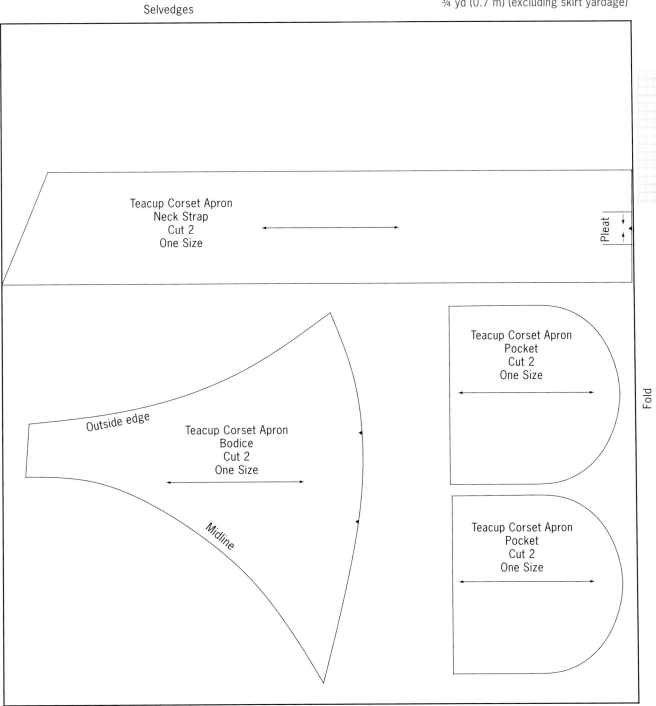

Teacup Corset Apron
Neck Strap
Cut 2
One Size

Pleat

Teacup Corset Apron
Pocket
Cut 2
One Size

Outside edge

Teacup Corset Apron
Bodice
Cut 2
One Size

Midline

Teacup Corset Apron
Pocket
Cut 2
One Size

Fold

Selvedges

Little Chef Apron and Hat Top

44–45" (112–114.5 cm) main

1¾ yd (1.6 m)

Note: The Apron and Hat shown are cut from a directional print fabric. If you are using a directional print or a fabric with a nap (p. 152), be sure to place all pieces facing the same direction, as shown in the layout diagram.

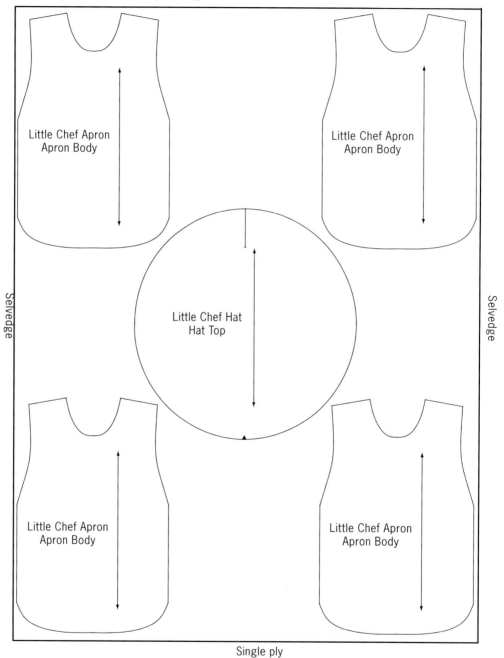

Petit Artiste Smock

44"–45" (112–114.5 cm) fabric

1¼ yd (1.14 m)

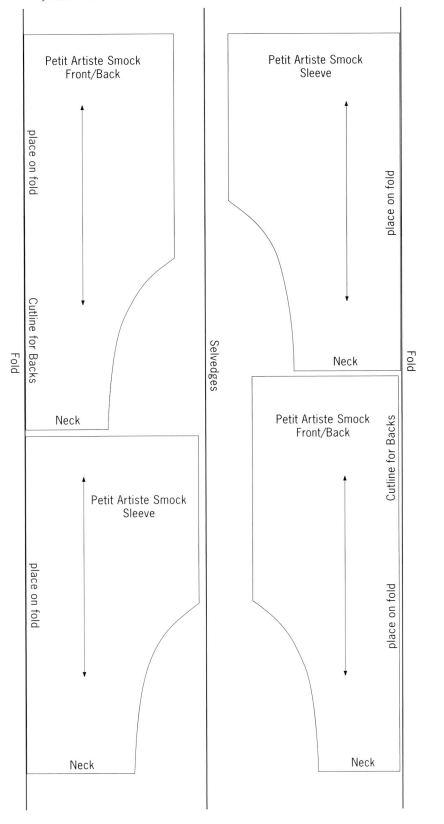

aPPLiQUÉ PRIMER

This chapter provides you with all of the tips and tricks you will need in order to start appliquéing with confidence. I suggest that you read through the chapter, visit your local fabric store to pick up any special materials that you might need, and sit down with a piece of linen fabric and your scraps to try out a few of the techniques described. Try some circles, move on to a leaf or a bird, and see what evolves on your piece of linen. The practice will help you get comfortable with the techniques and you can always use this "appliqué doodle" to embellish a special project later on. I will outline a few appliqué techniques in the following pages to get you started, but there are many more options available than those I am able to include here. Check the Resources on p. 158 for suggestions on where to look for more information on appliqué.

ORGANIZING YOUR SCRAPS AND FINDING FABRIC

We can follow the example of the generations of women before us who treasured (and used) every scrap of fabric they owned to mend clothing, make warm quilts, and to fashion family heirlooms. Part of the beauty of appliqué is its inherent thriftiness— you just know that one day, you'll find a use for those odds and ends, so you stash them away. The problem is that you often keep them in that exact spot for years and soon you've got a monster scrap pile! It's okay—take a deep breath. The solution that worked for me was to organize my scraps by color using recycled canning jars for storage. Of course, this did involve a tortuous hour or so of sorting through my grocery bags of accumulated scraps, but in the end, it made me into a much happier crafter.

Finding New Fabric

If you are new to sewing or you have not yet accumulated quite such a mountain of scraps, you have several options for finding small pieces of fabric for your appliqués.

First, make a trip to your local fabric or quilting store to look for one of these:

Scrap Bag: A reasonably priced bag of scraps, usually the byproduct of factory production.

Jelly Roll: A "wheel" comprised of forty 2½" × 44" (6.5 × 112 cm) pieces of fabric in a certain colorway.

Fat Quarter: An 18" × 22" (45.5 × 56 cm) cut of quilting cotton. Sometimes, fabric stores and online fabric retailers will sell packets of fat quarters in coordinating colors.

If you are looking for some alternatives, consider the opportunities offered on the Internet. Quilters love getting rid of their fabric scraps and remnants on Ebay and you can also join your local Freecycle.org group for a cost-free fabric-hunting alternative. Why not try asking friends or relatives if they might have any forgotten bags of fabric in their closets or attics? Many people will be ecstatic to have you take them off their hands!

Choosing the Right Appliqué Fabrics

When searching for the perfect scraps for appliqué work, it's best to have 100% medium-weight cotton. While appliqué work can be done with virtually any fabric, such as silk, polyester, and rayon, you will have to use different stitching and fabric care methods.

Most importantly, think of what your appliqué will become—will it be an accent on a piece of clothing or a much-used blanket, or will it be framed and remain untouched on a wall? You can use any fabric on a project that won't need to be washed, while projects that include beading, embroidery, or other delicate details may need to be gently washed by hand. If, however, your project will necessitate frequent washing, it's best to stick with 100% cotton with a high thread count (the number of lengthwise and crosswise threads per square inch). Remember to prewash any fabrics that will be made into a project that you anticipate washing in the future; this will allow you to prevent unsightly puckering caused by shrinkage during subsequent washings.

Choosing the Right Background Fabric

When choosing your background fabric, look for something that has a thread count similar to or greater than that of your appliqué scraps. Medium-weight linen, wool suiting, silk douppioni, linen/cotton blends, and 100% cotton fabrics are some that work very well. Certain types of appliqué work also look great on velvet, velveteen, or corduroy—just be prepared to use a machine appliqué technique instead of hand appliqué for these types of thicker fabrics. Finally, if you are choosing a knitted fabric for your appliqué project, it's best to choose a medium-weight cotton jersey or bamboo knit. Anything with a high percentage of synthetic fiber (such as rayon or spandex) might be a bit too slinky to stand up to appliqué.

APPLIQUÉ PREPARATION

Here is what you need to know in order to prepare all of your materials for appliqué.

Preparing Appliqué Templates

There are many techniques for preparing and finishing appliqués using either a raw or turned edge and a variety of hand and machine stitches. Some projects will dictate the method you choose, but in many cases you will be able to choose the one you prefer. I suggest that you try out a few of the techniques outlined in the following pages. You will learn which ones you prefer and the pros and cons of each.

Tips

- Always have both craft and fabric scissors on hand when preparing templates. Use the craft scissors to cut the template material (such as template plastic or freezer paper) because they can make your fabric scissors dull. Reserve your precious fabric scissors for cutting fabric; they will stay sharper longer.

- All of the suggested template materials (template plastic, freezer paper, and paper-backed fusible web) should be sufficiently see-through to simply place them on top of the templates to trace the shapes.

- Fine-tipped permanent markers can be used to draw on most template materials. I have found Micron fine-tipped pens to be excellent for use on many of them; however, a fine-tipped Sharpie seems to work best when drawing on template plastic.

- If you will be using your template to trace directly onto the front or back of the fabric itself (as in certain hand-appliqué techniques as well as reverse appliqué), make sure you place the fabric on a surface that is hard but not slippery. Fine sandpaper or a self-healing rotary mat will work.

Preparing Unfinished-Edge Appliqué

The unfinished-edge techniques are pretty quick and they are also a little easier to use with appliqués that have more intricate edges, which would be difficult to turn under.

Paper-Backed Fusible Web

The paper-backed fusible web method is quick and easy, allowing you to secure the appliqué in place for stitching. It leaves a raw edge that you can easily cover with a variety of beautiful stitches, and it works well for both large and small pieces, particularly for designs that have an elaborate edge.

figure 1

TOOLS AND MATERIALS:

    Paper-backed fusible web

    Iron and ironing board

    Craft scissors

    Fabric scissors

    Embroidery scissors

    Fine-tipped permanent marker or pencil

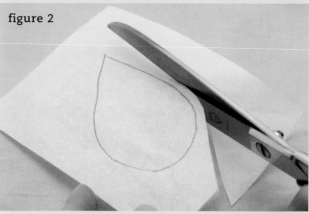

figure 2

1 Place fusible web directly over the template with the paper side facing up. Trace the template using a fine-tipped permanent marker or pencil (**figure 1**).

2 Cut out the shape, leaving an allowance of about ¼" (6 mm) around the edge (**figure 2**).

3 Place the fusible web, fusible side down, onto the wrong side of the appliqué fabric and follow the manufacturer's instructions to fuse the web to the fabric with your iron. Let cool.

4 Cut along the pencil markings on the paper backing (**figure 3**). Remove the paper backing just before you are ready to fuse the appliqué to the background fabric.

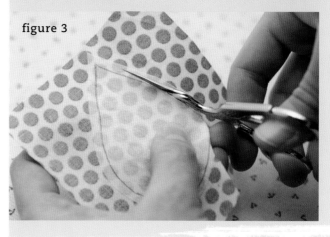

figure 3

stitching recommendations:

    Blanket stitch (p. 146)

    Blind hem/Invisible stitch (p. 146)

    Satin stitch (p. 147)

    Straight stitch (p. 146)

    Zigzag stitch (p. 147)

BASIC TEMPLATE MATERIALS

See the techniques on pp. 136–145 when deciding on what materials to use. Do some experimenting; eventually you will find what works best for you.

Freezer Paper

This heavyweight paper (a kitchen staple for many years) has a waxy coating on one side only—the other side is wax-free (this is not to be confused with wax paper). If you are unsuccessful in finding a roll in the grocery store near the aluminum foil, check at your local fabric store or search for it online. I recommend buying Quilter's Freezer Paper Sheets made by C & T Publishing. These 8½" × 11" (21.5 × 28 cm) sheets can be fed through ink jet printers. This is particularly handy when you've downloaded a template that you've found online because you can just print the design directly onto the paper side of the sheet.

Freezer Paper

Template Plastic

Template Plastic

Template plastic, like freezer paper, is translucent, making it easy to transfer a template design with a fine-tipped permanent marker. I tend to use template plastic because it works well for the Template Plastic and Starch Method for turning under appliqué edges, as well as being durable and tear-resistant, therefore extending the life of your templates through multiple uses. If you will be exposing the template plastic to heat, such as for turned edge appliqué preparation methods that require ironing over the plastic itself, be sure to get heat-resistant template plastic. Be cautious, however, when ironing onto the plastic. It's heat-resistant, not heat-proof. Turn your iron to a much lower setting when working with this stuff, or you will cause the plastic to warp.

Paper-Backed Fusible Web

While it has a reputation as a sticky character, paper-backed fusible web has single-handedly revolutionized appliqué. To use it, you simply trace the appliqué outline directly onto the paper side, fuse the sticky side to the wrong side of the fabric, cut out the design, remove the paper backing, and affix it to the background fabric with your iron. The appliqué is now ready to be stitched, and it will not slip around. When you use paper-backed fusible web, you'll have no need for pins.

Frayed Raw Edge

This is, hands down, the easiest method of appliqué out there. Use it when you want to show off the frayed edges of a lovely linen fabric.

TOOLS AND MATERIALS:

Template plastic, freezer paper, or paper-backed fusible web

Fine-tipped permanent marker or pencil (pencil can only be used with fusible web)

Iron and ironing board (for use with fusible web only)

Craft scissors

Fabric scissors

TIP: If you will be handsewing around the edge of the appliqué, be sure that you make small stitches or else the fabric might continue to fray beyond the stitchline.

1 Trace the appliqué template onto template plastic, freezer paper (nonwaxy side), or paper-backed fusible web (paper side) and cut out.

2 Place the template onto the wrong side of your appliqué fabric and trace around it (or fuse the fusible web

according to manufacturer's instructions). Cut out the shape with fabric scissors, leaving a ⅛" (3 mm) allowance beyond the traced line (**figure 1**).

3 Place the appliqué onto the background fabric, right side up, and sew it in place, ⅛" (3 mm) from the edge. Pick out some threads along the edges or rub the fabric between your fingers to fray the edges slightly.

stitching recommendations:

Straight stitch (p. 146)

Zigzag stitch (p. 147)

Any decorative stitch made either by hand or machine (see p. 148–151 for some hand-embroidery options)

Preparing Turned-Edge Appliqué

There are several options when preparing appliqués for a turned-edge finishing technique. These will give you a nice, finished edge that won't fray.

Lightweight Fusible Interfacing

This is a brilliant technique I learned from a tutorial on Purlsoho.com's blog, The Purl Bee. It is best for large appliqué shapes that don't have an intricate edge. The fusible interfacing will give you a crisp turned-under edge as well as holding the appliqué in place as you stitch. You can use muslin, instead of fusible interfacing, for this technique. However, if you choose to use muslin, you'll need to pin the appliqué securely to the background fabric to stitch it in place.

TOOLS AND MATERIALS:

Template plastic or freezer paper

Fine-tipped permanent marker

Erasable fabric marking pen or tailor's chalk

Lightweight fusible interfacing

Embroidery or other small scissors

Craft scissors

Iron and ironing board

Point turner (optional)

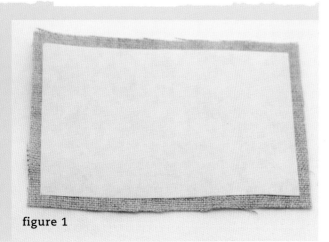

figure 1

1 Use the fine-tipped permanent marker to trace your appliqué template onto template plastic or freezer paper and cut it out. Place the template onto the wrong side of your appliqué fabric and trace around it with an erasable fabric marking pen or tailor's chalk (**figure 1**).

2 Cut out the shape, leaving a ¼" (6 mm) seam allowance around the edges.

3 Place the cut appliqué fabric, right side down, onto the fusible side of the lightweight fusible interfacing (**figure 2**). Cut the interfacing to the same shape as the appliqué. Pin the two together.

4 Sew a straight stitch along the entire line that you made in step 1 (**figure 3**). Using the embroidery scissors, clip the corners (p. 156) and clip along any curves (p. 156).

5 Cut a slit in the middle of the interfacing only (be careful not to cut through the fabric) just large enough to turn the appliqué.

6 Turn the appliqué right side out through the slit and use a point turner, knitting needle, or other tool to push out the edges and corners, being careful not to tear the interfacing (**figure 4**).

7 Finger-press along the edges of the appliqué and then fuse it to the background fabric according to manufacturer's instructions (for the fusible interfacing). Secure with pins along the edges just to be sure that the fabric won't shift during stitching.

stitching recommendations:

Blanket stitch (p. 146)

Blind hem/Invisible stitch (p. 146)

Satin stitch (p. 147)

Straight stitch (p. 146)

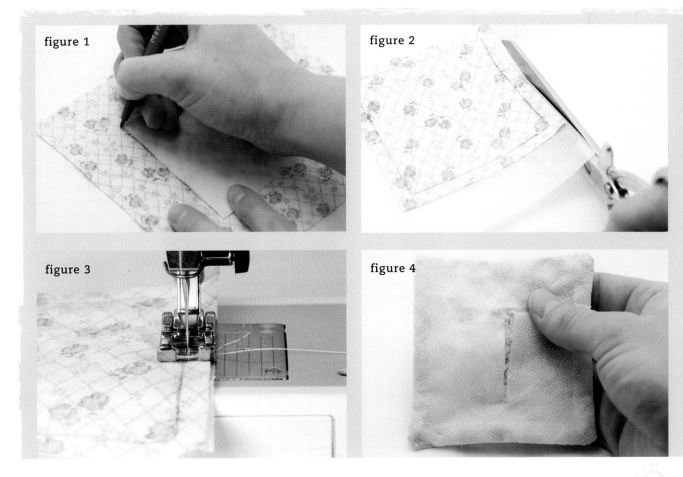

figure 1

figure 2

figure 3

figure 4

Freezer Paper and Glue Stick

This method produces a delectably smooth, turned-under edge, but requires a bit of time and patience.

TOOLS AND MATERIALS:

- Freezer paper
- Fine-tipped permanent marker or pencil
- Iron and ironing board
- Embroidery or other small scissors
- Craft scissors
- Fabric scissors
- Acid-free glue stick
- Spray bottle with water

1 Lay the freezer paper onto the appliqué template with the shiny (waxy) side facing up and trace the shape using a fine-tipped permanent marker or pencil; cut out.

2 Use your iron to fuse the freezer paper, waxy side down, onto the wrong side of your appliqué fabric. Cut the fabric around the freezer paper template, leaving a ¼" (6 mm) allowance around the shape (**figure 1**).

3 Using your embroidery scissors, clip any concave curves to about ⅛" (3 mm) from the edge of the freezer paper (**figure 2**). Any concave points (such as the space between 2 flower petals) should be clipped as close as possible to the freezer paper.

4 With a glue stick, apply glue to the entire ¼" (6 mm) fabric allowance (on the wrong side). Slowly, repositioning when necessary, use your index finger and thumb to press the allowance over the edge of the freezer paper (**figure 3**). If you need to turn the allowance over a sharp point, start by folding the fabric over the point, then pressing over the fabric on each side, one by one.

5 Let the glue dry, then place the appliqué onto the background fabric, right side up, and stitch completely around the appliqué to secure it in place.

6 Flip over the appliquéd area so that the wrong side of the background fabric is facing you. Cut out the background fabric along the inside edge of the appliqué stitching, leaving a ¼" (6 mm) allowance. With the background fabric removed, you will be looking at the freezer paper. Use a small spray bottle containing water to slightly moisten the freezer paper from the back of the appliqué, along the stitching. Remove the paper. You should now be able to see the wrong side of the appliqué.

stitching recommendation:

Blind hem/Invisible stitch (p. 146)

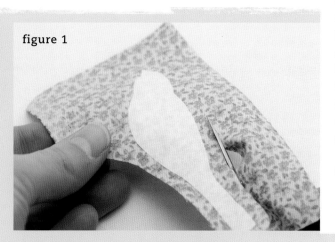

figure 1

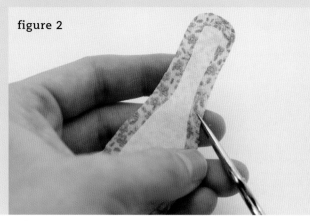

figure 2

figure 3

Template Plastic and Starch

This is my personal favorite! I find that this method keeps your edges securely turned under, making it ideal for appliquéing on the go, since you have the option of handstitching the shapes to the background fabric.

TOOLS AND MATERIALS

- Heat-resistant template plastic
- Fine-tipped permanent marker
- Embroidery or other small scissors
- Craft scissors
- Fabric scissors
- Liquid starch and small paintbrush
- Erasable fabric marking pen or tailor's chalk

1 Using the fine-tipped permanent marker, trace your appliqué template onto heat-resistant template plastic and cut it out.

2 Place the template plastic onto the wrong side of the appliqué fabric. Use an erasable fabric marking pen or tailor's chalk to trace around it and then cut out, leaving a ¼" (6 mm) allowance beyond the traced line.

3 Using the embroidery scissors, clip any convex curves to about ⅛" (3 mm) from the marked line (**figure 1**). Any concave points (such as the space between 2 flower petals) should be clipped as close as possible to the marked line.

4 In a small dish, dilute a small amount of liquid starch with equal parts water and mix it together. Use a small paintbrush to apply the starch to the entire ¼" (6 mm) allowance (on the wrong side; **figure 2**).

5 Place the plastic template onto the wrong side of the fabric (centered in the marked lines so that the ¼" [6 mm] allowance is left free) and press the fabric allowances over the template with the tip of your iron. On any conxev curves you will form small pleats in the fabric with the iron so that the fabric folds smoothly over the template edge (**figure 3**).

6 To make a sharp point, press the fabric allowance directly over the tip of the template (**figure 4**, page 142),

figure 1

figure 2

figure 3

then press over the fabric, first on one side, then the other, kind of like wrapping a present (**figure 5**, page 142).

7 Once you have pressed all of the fabric allowances over the template plastic, flip the appliqué over and

figure 4

figure 5

figure 6

press on the right side of the fabric. Let cool, then re-move the template plastic, and press again to make sure that the folded edges stay in place (**figure 6**).

stitching recommendations:

Blanket stitch (p. 146)

Blind hem/Invisible stitch (p. 146)

Standard hand-appliqué stitch (p. 149)

Zigzag stitch (p. 147)

Preparing a Circle

Here's a foolproof way of making perfect circles to appliqué.

TOOLS AND MATERIALS:

Heat-resistant template plastic

Fine-tipped permanent marker

Craft scissors

Fabric Scissors

Erasable fabric marking pen or tailor's chalk

Handsewing needle and thread

Liquid starch and small paintbrush or spray bottle (optional)

Iron and ironing board

1 Trace the circle directly onto the template plastic us-ing the permanent marker and then cut out using craft scissors (if you do not have a template available for the desired size, look around your house for something to trace, like a jar lid or a small bowl).

2 Place your plastic circle template onto the wrong side of the appliqué fabric and trace around it with a fabric marking pen or tailor's chalk. Cut out the circle, leaving a ¼" (6 mm) allowance beyond the traced line (**figure 1**).

3 Thread a handsewing needle with thread and tie a knot at the end. Use a running stitch (p. 153) to sew along the edge of the circle, equidistant between the fabric's edge and the traced line (**figure 2**). Do not tie off.

4 Place the circle right side down and center the plastic template on the wrong side. Gently tug on the thread to gather the fabric around the edge of the plastic template. Take a few more stitches around the edges to tack the fabric in place. Use your fingers to smooth out the edge and ensure that the gathers are evenly distributed around the plastic template (see **figure 3**).

5 If you'd like, apply some diluted liquid starch to the turned-under edges of the circle using either a spray bottle or a small paint brush (**figure 3**); let dry.

6 Using low heat, press along the edges of the circle with an iron (**figure 4**). Remove the gathering stitches and the plastic template. Ensure that the turned-under edges are in place and then press again.

stitching recommendations:

Any stitch, machine or hand (see pp. 146–147 for machine-stitching options, and pp. 149–151 for handstitching options)

figure 1

figure 2

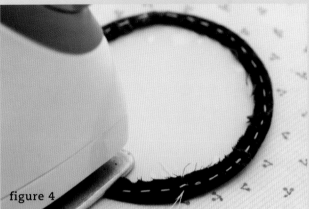

figure 3

figure 4

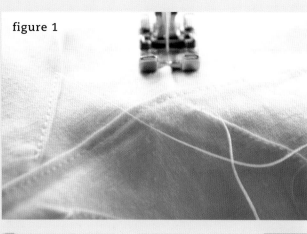

figure 1

figure 2

Dimensional Shapes

Dimensional shapes really add a stunning element to a project. The good news is that they're easy to make, and when you work with them, your creativity need know no bounds. All you have to do is think of a shape, draw it, and (at times) get a little wild with your iron.

TOOLS AND MATERIALS:

Template plastic

Fine-tipped permanent marker

Erasable fabric marking pen or tailor's chalk

Iron (or mini iron) and ironing board

Point turner or other turning tool like a knitting needle

1 If you are creating your own shape, draw it on a piece of paper first. Trace your chosen design onto template plastic with a permanent marker.

2 Decide if you want to add any special pleats to your fabric to create a special effect, such as the veins in a leaf (as seen in the Patchwork Placemats on p. 15); otherwise, skip to Step 3. Cut a piece of your appliqué fabric with plenty of room to spare (for example, if your design's dimensions are 2" × 3" [5 × 7.5 cm] at widest points, cut out a rectangle of fabric that is about 4" × 5" [10 × 12.5 cm]). Create the pleats where you would like them by pinching the fabric to create a fold and then press each in place with your iron (a mini iron can be used). Anchor the pleats by machine-stitching along the base of each one (**figure 1**). Press once again.

3 Place the plastic template onto the wrong side of your appliqué fabric and trace with a fabric pen or tailor's chalk. If you've ironed in some dimensional details, make sure they are appropriately placed as you trace (**figure 2**). Cut out the shape, leaving a ¼" (6 mm) seam allowance beyond the traced line.

4 Repeat Step 3 to trace the template onto the wrong side of another piece of appliqué fabric (this one should be free of dimensional details; be sure to flip the template over if the shape is not the same on both sides) and cut. You now have two appliqué shapes which should match up perfectly.

5 Place the two pieces with right sides together and pin (**figure 3**). Sew along the marked line, leaving a 1½" (3.8 cm) opening for turning (don't forget to backtack [p. 152] at the beginning and end of the stitch line). It's best if the opening is left on a fairly straight portion of the appliqué.

6 Turn the appliqué right side out and use a point turner or other turning tool to smooth out the edges and push out any corners. Tuck in the seam allowances at the opening, finger-press, and slipstitch (p. 154) closed (**figure 4**).

TIP: If you want a poofier appliqué, like the circle (tree) on the Bird in Hand Laptop Bag (p. 49), fill the shape with a bit of stuffing before you stitch the opening closed. Don't get too happy with your stuffing, though, or else stitching the appliqué to the background could end up being an arduous task!

stitching recommendations:

Standard hand-appliqué stitch (p. 149)

Straight stitch (p. 146)

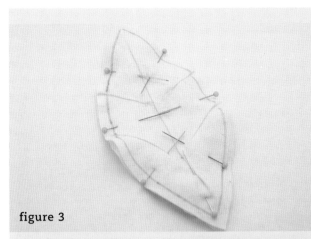
figure 3

figure 4

ATTACHING AND EMBELLISHING APPLIQUÉ

Many different stitches can be used to attach and embellish appliqué, as well as to embellish other parts of a project.

There are several options to choose from when you are attaching appliqué to a background fabric and some of the options are also great embellishment. Read through the options for attaching appliqué by machine and hand to determine the best option for your project, then take a look at the Embroidery Stitch Library on p. 150 for a variety of stitches that can be done by hand to embellish appliqué or background fabrics.

Machine Stitching to Attach and Embellish Appliqué

Consult your sewing machine manual to find out if your machine has the following stitches and for information on settings and how to use them. If you are unfamiliar with a stitch, it's a good idea to practice on

BEGINNING AND ENDING MACHINE APPLIQUÉ STITCHES

Take one stitch, then raise the needle and pull both the top thread and the loop of bobbin thread out and to one side. Pulling the bobbin thread to the side will prevent unsightly knots from forming on the back of the fabric. Continue stitching until you have sewn around the entire edge of the appliqué.

To finish stitching, reduce the length of the stitch drastically (to 0.3–0.4 mm) and take a few tiny stitches just over the beginning stitches, which will lock all of them in place. Raise the needle and the presser foot, pull the threads to the side, and clip them right at the fabric edge with your embroidery scissors.

scrap fabric and experiment with thread color, stitch size, and placement before applying it to your project.

Straight Stitch

Thread recommendations: Any sewing thread you have on hand (such as all-purpose mercerized cotton or silk thread). Monofilament/invisible thread if you want the stitching to blend in.

The straight stitch is the standard stitch on your sewing machine and can be used to embellish and embroider both raw-edge and turned-edge appliqué, using the standard stitch length (2.5 mm) or a longer stitch length (see your sewing machine manual for assistance). Use a straight-stitch presser foot, an open-toe embroidery foot, or, preferably, a blind-hem foot. Using a blind-hem foot will help you to keep the stitching at an even distance from the edge of the appliqué (as long as the appliqué's edges are not too curvy).

Blind-Hem/Invisible Stitch

Thread recommendations: A monofilament/invisible thread for the top thread and a 60-weight cotton or polyester thread in a color to match your fabric in the bobbin.

A blind hem is a great option for attaching turned-edge appliqué to background fabric as it is virtually invisible (this one won't work with raw-edge appliqué). Begin by setting both the stitch width and length to 1 mm and then adjust as necessary (you want the stitches to be small enough to be virtually invisible, but large enough to catch both the background and appliqué fabric). Use the blind-hem foot and place the presser foot guide against the edge of the appliqué so that the stitches will catch just the edge of the appliqué fabric.

Blanket Stitch

Thread recommendation: A 50-weight or thicker cotton embroidery thread (I like to use a color that contrasts with my fabric so that the stitch stands out).

A blanket stitch can be used on wool felt, turned-edge, and raw-edge (with fusible web) appliqués. Use an open-toe embroidery foot and make sure that the right swing of the needle falls next to the edge of the appliqué on the background fabric.

Zigzag Stitch

Thread recommendations: A 60-weight cotton embroidery thread or a 40-weight rayon or polyester thread in a color to match or complement your fabric. Monofilament/invisible thread if you want the stitching to blend in.

A zigzag stitch is a great option for raw-edge (with fusible web) and turned-edge appliqués. I've found that using a .75 mm stitch length and a 1.5 mm stitch width are ideal for attaching appliqué to fabric, but you should do some experimenting to find out what works best for you. When attaching appliqué to a background fabric, the right swing of the needle should fall just off the edge of the appliqué to secure it in place on the background fabric.

TIP: Use an open-toe embroidery foot if you have one. This foot makes it easy to see the edge of the appliqué and will help you to make neat stitches right at the appliqué edge.

Satin Stitch

Thread recommendations: 60-weight cotton embroidery thread or 50-weight rayon or polyester thread

A satin stitch provides the ideal finish for any high-use project that will need to be washed often, such as clothing. It's decorative as well as sturdy. Keep your frustration level low by using a satin stitch only with unfinished edge appliqués—you can use it for appliqués with turned-under edges, but this gets to be pretty bulky and cumbersome. I recommend sticking to a 1.5 mm stitch width and a 0.2 mm stitch length, adjusting as necessary. Position the needle and presser foot so that the needle's right swing will come down just off the edge of the appliqué and the left swing will come down onto the appliqué itself.

Straight Stitch

Zigzag Stitch

Blanket Stitch

Satin Stitch

TIPS: You'll need a temporary stabilizer in order to machine appliqué using a satin stitch. I prefer using a sheet of tear-away stabilizer that I can cut slightly larger than the size of my appliqué and pin to the wrong side of the background fabric. After stitching through all the layers, carefully tear the stabilizer away from the wrong side of the background fabric. If you skip the stabilizer, you are likely to end up with a bunched or pulled fabric around the satin stitching. Always begin stitching along a straighter edge of the appliqué to make maneuvering easier.

Handstitching to Attach Appliqué

I recommend using a size 11 Sharps needle. If you would like something shorter, experiment with a Betweens and if you would like something longer, try a Straw needle.

Handstitching (and embroidery) is often much easier if you place the background fabric in an embroidery hoop to hold it taut as you stitch.

Thread your needle with an 18–20" (45.5–51 cm) length of thread (see p. 10 for information on choosing the right thread). Knot the end of the thread securely (my favorite knot is the quilter's knot, also called a "magic knot" or an "Australian knot").

Quilter's Knot

1 Thread the needle and then grasp the eye of the needle with the thumb and forefinger of your nondominant hand. Bring the long end of the thread up so that the point of the needle and the end of the thread are facing each other and then slip the end of the thread between the fingers that are holding the eye of the needle (you now have a loop of thread hanging from the needle; **figure 1**).

2 With your free hand, wrap the tail of the longer thread around the needle 3 times (**figure 2**).

3 Slide the wound thread down and lodge it between the fingers holding the eye of the needle and then, with your free hand, slowly pull the needle from the pointed end (**figure 3**) until the entire length of thread has passed through your thumb and forefinger (still grasping the wound thread). The wound thread will form a small knot at the base of the thread.

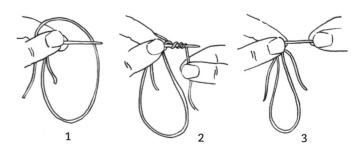

1   2   3

Once you have completed your handstitching, you'll need to tie off your thread securely. I recommend using the following knot:

Finishing Knot

1. Insert your needle into the background fabric where you would take your next stitch. Flip over the background fabric so the wrong side is facing you, and pull the thread completely through to the wrong side; hold the needle close to the background fabric and wind the thread around the needle three times (**figure 1**).

2. Keeping the thread wound around the needle, insert the tip of the needle as close as possible to your last stitch in between the background fabric and the appliqué fabric (**figure 2**). Your needle should not poke through the appliqué fabric on the right side. Pivot the needle tip and bring it back through to the wrong side of the background fabric, about ½" (1.3 cm) from where you inserted it. Pull the needle so that the working thread comes through the wound thread, forming a small knot (**figure 3**).

Give the thread a slight tug to pop the knot through the background fabric so that it is in between the background and appliqué fabrics, keeping it out of sight. Cut the remaining thread with your embroidery scissors as close to the background fabric as possible.

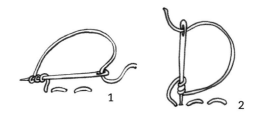

1   2

3

STANDARD HAND-APPLIQUÉ STITCH

Pin or secure your appliqué in place on the background fabric.

Push the threaded needle up from the wrong side of the background fabric at 1 so that it passes through the folded-under appliqué edge, catching a few woven threads of the appliqué. Pull the thread all the way through so that it is on top of the fabric, then push the needle point through the background fabric almost exactly where you just stitched, at 2. Hold the needle parallel to the edge of the appliqué and bring the needle tip up about ⅛" (3 mm) from where you first inserted the point, at 3. Continue stitching in this manner, pulling the thread so that it remains taut yet not so much that it causes the fabric to pucker.

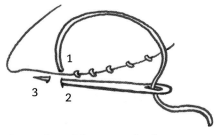

Hand-Embroidery Stitches

Hand embroidery is a wonderful way to embellish your projects and because it doesn't require the use of a sewing machine, you can do it almost anywhere! Use cotton embroidery thread or embroidery floss and experiment with the number of strands used for more or less visual impact.

For information on threading and knotting, see Handstitching to Attach Appliqué at left.

With embroidery, you have the option of tracing and transferring a design to your fabric and using the lines as your stitching guide, or freehand "doodling" with your thread. I'll provide you with the basics and some tips to help you get started. If you end up getting addicted like I did, check out the Resources on p. 158 for extra embroidery inspiration.

Transferring Designs to Your Fabric

If you plan to use a machine stitch or a hand-embroidery technique to create a design on a project, you'll need to transfer your design to the fabric so that you have a guideline to follow as you stitch.

If your background fabric is thin enough, your best bet for transferring an embroidery design is a source of light, masking tape, and a very thin permanent marker. I suggest taking the templates in the back of the book and copying them onto basic white printer paper (If you have a copy machine at home, just make a black and white copy—if not, place a piece of white paper on top of the template and use a pen to trace along the lines). Take the copy or tracing and tape it to a window pane. Tape your fabric to the window pane with the right side of the fabric facing you, over the copy or tracing. Use a very fine-tipped permanent marker or pen (such as a Micron pen) or an erasable fabric marking pen (if the marks won't be completely covered by embroidery) to trace over the design and onto your fabric.

If your fabric is too thick for easy tracing, you'll need to use transfer paper (I suggest using Saral transfer paper in white for dark fabrics or graphite for light fabrics; see Resources). Simply copy or trace your design onto a piece of regular white paper as before and stack the materials as follows: background fabric with right side facing up, transfer paper with carbon side down, and paper with pattern design facing up. Use a ballpoint pen to trace over the design, pressing firmly so that the carbon transfers onto the fabric.

EMBROIDERY STITCH LIBRARY

Chain Stitch

Working from top to bottom, bring the needle up at 1 and reinsert at 1 to create a loop; do not pull the thread taut. Bring the needle up at 2, through the loop, and gently pull the needle toward you to pull the loop flush with the fabric. Repeat by reinserting at 2 to create another loop and bring the needle up at 3. To finish a row of stitches, tack down the last loop with a short running stitch (p. 151).

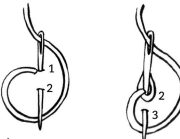

Backstitch

Working from right to left, bring the needle up at 1 and insert behind your starting point at 2. Bring the needle up at 3. Repeat by inserting at 1 and then bring the needle up one stitch length beyond 3.

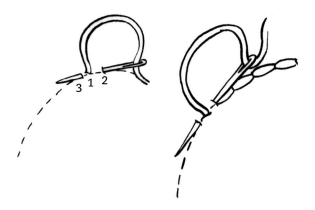

Couching

Working from right to left, use one thread, known as the couching or working thread, to tack down one or more laid threads or yarns (leave a tail of about 6" [15 cm] of the laid thread or yarn). Bring the working thread up at 1, insert at 2, and bring up at 3 (about ½" [1.3 cm] to the left of 2). When finished, leave a tail of about 6" (15 cm) on the laid thread or yarn and use a tapestry needle to bring it to the wrong side of the fabric, then tie off and trim. Repeat at the other end of the laid thread or yarn.

Blanket Stitch

Working from left to right, bring the needle up at 1 and insert at 2. Bring back up at 3 and over the working thread. Repeat. When using blanket stitch around the edge of an appliqué, be sure that the bottom of the stitches butt up against the edge of the appliqué.

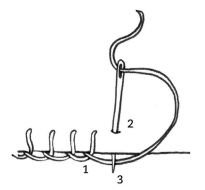

French Knot

Bring the needle up at 1 and hold the thread taut about 2" (5 cm) above the fabric. Point the needle toward your fingers and wrap the thread tautly around the needle twice. Insert the needle into the fabric near 1 and complete the knot by holding the thread taut near the wrapped thread as you pull the needle toward the wraps and through the fabric.

TIP: Work with three strands of embroidery floss to make full yet manageable knots.

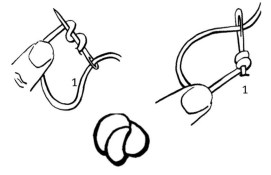

Running Stitch

Working from left to right, bring the needle up and insert at 1, ⅛–¼"(3–6 mm)" from the starting point. Bring the needle up at 2 (⅛–¼" [3–6 mm] to the left of 1) and repeat.

TIP: Use a wool yarn (such as Paternayan Persian) or 4–6 strands of cotton embroidery floss to draw the eye to the stitching.

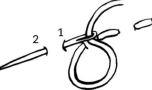

Satin Stitch

Generally worked from left to right, satin stitch is most often used to fill in a shape or create a thick, scallop-like edge. Bring the needle up at 1, insert at 2, and bring back up at 3. Repeat.

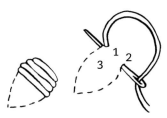

Split Stitch

Working from left to right, bring the needle up at 1 and insert the needle ⅛–¼" (3–6 mm) away at 2; bring the needle up through the center of the previous stitch, at 3 (you will split the threads with your needle). When working with multiple strands you can insert the needle between the strands instead of splitting the thread.

TIP: Use two strands of embroidery floss for a very delicate stitch or four strands for more visibility.

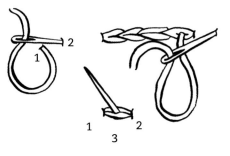

Stem Stitch

Working from left to right, bring the needle up at 1 and insert the needle ⅛–¼" (3–6 mm) away at 2. Bring the needle up halfway between 1 and 2, at 3. Keeping the newly created loop below the needle and stitchline, pull the stitch taut. Continue by inserting the needle ⅛–¼" (3–6 mm) to the right of 2, then bring up the needle to the right of 2.

glossary

TERMS

Backtack: Sewing backward over previous machine stitching to secure it in place. This is usually done at the beginning and end of a stitch line. Most sewing machines have a backtack function; refer to your sewing machine manual for assistance with the settings on your machine.

Baste: Uses long, loose running/straight stitches to temporarily secure a seam or other feature (such as gathers) in place by hand or by machine. The longer length makes the stitches easier to remove when they are no longer needed. To **machine-baste**, set your machine to a long stitch length; to **hand-baste**, use long running stitches, spaced about ¼" (6 mm) apart.

Bias: The bias of a fabric is located at a 45-degree angle to the lengthwise grain. It has a higher stretch than the straight grain in either the lengthwise or crosswise direction and is also characterized by a very fluid drape.

Drape: A term that refers to the aesthetics of a fabric, specifically how it hangs from an object or body.

Ease/Ease in: If a pattern instructs you to "ease" or "ease in," you are sewing a longer section of fabric to a shorter section as smoothly as possible and without causing tucks or gathers in your seam. To ease a longer section of fabric, pin together the ends or the notches evenly, as instructed by the pattern, then continue to pin the two sections together, keeping the edges even and gently forcing the excess fabric of the longer section away from the edge. You may have to stretch the shorter piece slightly to accommodate the longer piece, but don't stretch too much or you may cause the fabric to warp and the finished shape may be uneven. Use a lot of pins and go slowly as you sew the sections together, regularly checking for tucks and smoothing any bubbles in the fabric away from the seamline.

Edgestitch: A line of machine stitching that is placed very close to an edge or existing seamline, usually no more than ⅟₁₆–⅛" (2–3 mm) away.

Fabric grain: The threads in a woven fabric that crisscross each other at right angles along the length and width of the fabric. The **lengthwise grain** refers to the threads that run along the length, parallel to the selvdges; the **crosswise grain** refers to the threads that run along the width, perpendicular to the selvedges. Straight grain refers to cutting fabric along the lengthwise or crosswise grain.

Finger press: Pressing a crease or fold by pushing firmly with your fingers instead of using an iron.

French seam: A seam in which the raw edges are enclosed on both the right and wrong sides of the garment or project.

Grainline: A line marked on a pattern that is used to line up the pattern with the straight grain of a fabric (grainlines are used to line up a pattern on the lengthwise grain, unless specifically marked as crosswise).

Lining: Material used to hide the wrong side of a garment or project. Usually the lining is a mirror image of the shell.

Nap: Describes fabrics with a directional print or texture. Fabrics such as velvet and corduroy and knitted fabrics are examples of fabrics with a textural nap.

Notch: A pattern marking placed on the edge to indicate placement of an adjoining piece or other feature. Notches appear as small triangles against the edge of the pattern, with the point of the triangle facing in toward the pattern (see the Pattern Guide on p. 157).

Overlock stitch: A stitch used to finish the raw edges of fabric to prevent raveling, it can be produced with a serger. The zigzag stitch (p. 147) on a conventional sewing machine can be used as an alternative to finish the edges.

Raglan: A type of sleeve that features a diagonal seam extending to the collar, rather than a traditional armhole.

Raw edge: The cut edge of the fabric that has not yet been finished by seaming or hemming.

Right side: The right side of the fabric is the front side or the side that should be on the outside of a finished garment or project. On a print fabric, the print will be more visible on the right side of the fabric.

Running Stitch: This basic handstitch is made up of evenly spaced stitches and can vary in length according to the instruction or as desired. Running stitches are used for decorative purposes and/or for joining pieces by hand in some cases. See also Straight stitch.

Seam allowance: The fabric between the raw edge and the seam.

Selvedge: The tightly woven borders on the lengthwise edges of the fabric that are created by the weaving process.

Shell: The material on the outside of a garment or project.

Stitch in the ditch: Stitching directly over a previous stitch line.

Straight stitch: This basic stitch is the default stitch on your sewing machine and is used for most common sewing applications. See also Running Stitch.

Topstitch: Stitching that is visible on the outside of a garment or project that is used to provide extra stability and/or for decorative purposes.

Wale: A line that runs along the length of the fabric, created by the weave, such as the ribbing seen in corduroy fabric.

Wrong side: The underside of the fabric or the side that will be on the inside of a finished garment or project. On a print fabric, the print will be less visible on the wrong side of the fabric.

USEFUL STITCHES AND TECHNIQUES

Slipstitch

Take a stitch about ¼" (6 mm) long into the folded edge of one piece of fabric and then bring the needle out. Insert the needle into the folded edge of the opposite piece of fabric, directly across from the exit point of the thread in the previous stitch. Repeat by inserting the needle into the first piece of fabric, as before. This will create small, almost invisible stitches.

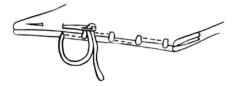

Whipstitch

Bring the needle up at 1 and insert at 2, then bring up at 3. The stitches can be as close together or as far apart as you wish.

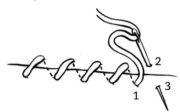

Double-Fold Binding

To figure out the width of strips to cut for double-fold binding, simply multiply the desired finished width of the binding by 4 and then add ⅛" (3 mm) for folding allowance.

Finished Binding Width	Cut Strip Width
¼" (6 mm)	1 ⅛" (2.8 cm)
½" (1.3 cm)	2 ⅛" (5.4 cm)
¾" (2 cm)	3 ⅛" (7.9 cm)
1" (2.5 cm)	4 ⅛" (10.5 cm)

Diagonal Seams for Joining Strips

Lay two strips, right sides together, at right angles. The area where the strips overlap forms a square. Sew diagonally across the square as shown below. Trim the excess fabric, ¼" (6 mm) from the seamline and press the seam allowances open. Repeat to join all the strips, forming one long fabric strip.

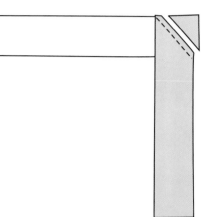

1 Cut the fabric strip(s) according to the chart at left and as directed by the instructions for either Bias or Straight Grain (p. 152) Binding (below). Cut a strip long enough to bind the project edge, or cut multiple strips and join them end to end according to the instructions under Diagonal Seams for Joining Strips at left. Be sure to remove the selvedges (p. 153) from the strips. Once the strips are prepared, follow Steps 2–4 at right to complete the binding.

Bias Binding: Fold one cut end of the fabric to meet one selvedge, forming a fold at a 45-degree angle to the selvedge (**figure 1**). With the fabric placed on a self-healing mat, cut off the fold with a rotary cutter, using a straight edge as a guide to make a straight cut. With the straight edge and rotary cutter, cut strips to the appropriate width (see chart at left; **figure 2**).

Straight Grain Binding: Cut strips across the width (crosswise grain [p. 152]) of the fabric, cutting them to the appropriate width (see chart at left).

2 Fold the strip in half lengthwise, with wrong sides together, allowing one raw edge to extend just past the other edge (about ¹⁄₁₆" [2 mm]), rather than folding it exactly in half; press. The slightly extended edge will make it easier to catch the bottom edge of the finished binding when it is sewn into place around the edge of a project.

3 Open up the fold and then fold each long edge toward the wrong side, so that the raw edges meet in the middle (**figure 3**).

4 Refold the binding along the existing center crease, enclosing the raw edges (**figure 4**), and press again.

Attaching Binding with Mitered Corners

1 Place the binding around the edge of the project, snugging the raw edge of the project up into the center crease of the binding. Be sure to place the slightly extended side of the binding on the bottom of the project (see Step 2 under Double Fold Binding at left). Pin the binding in place to the first corner.

2 Using your walking foot, topstitch (p. 153) the binding to the project a scant ¹⁄₈" (3 mm) from the binding's lower edges, stitching through all layers. As you sew along, check often to make sure that you are catching the edge of the binding on the bottom of the project as well. Continue sewing all the way to the first corner and backtack (p. 152). Remove the project from the machine and trim the threads (**figure 1**).

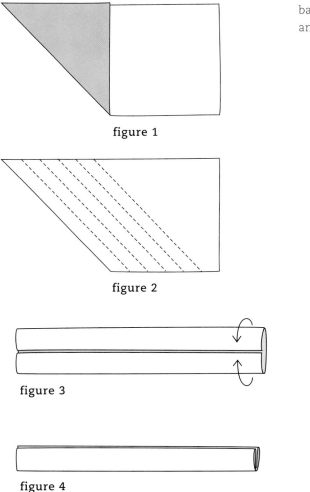

figure 1

figure 2

figure 3

figure 4

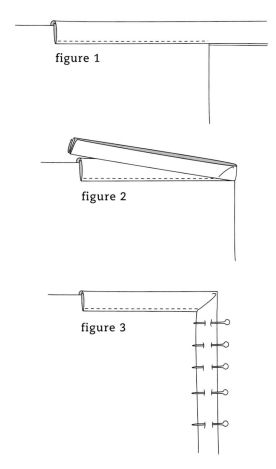

figure 1

figure 2

figure 3

3 From the first corner, fold the binding back on itself (the binding will turn inside out and begin to wrap around the already sewn binding). On both front and back, crease the binding diagonally near the corner as shown in **figure 2**; as you fold the binding back down, encase the adjoining raw edge (the binding will be right side out again) and pin in place (see **figure 3**).

4 Finger-press the resulting diagonal fold (miter) at the corner (**figure 3**).

5 Repeat Steps 2–4 to bind the remaining edges and miter the corners.

Clip the Corners

Clipping the corners of a project reduces bulk and allows for crisper corners in the finished product. To clip a corner, cut off a triangle-shaped piece of fabric, across the seam allowances at the corner. Cut close to the seamline, but be careful not to cut through the stitches.

Clip the Curves

Clipping the seam allowances along curved edges (concave or convex) reduces bulk and allows the seam to lie flat, eliminating puckering at the seamline. To clip the curves, make small, V-shaped cuts into the seam allowances along the curve (for concave curves, you can simply cut slits). Cut close to the seamline, but be careful not to cut through the stitches. Tighter curves will require more clipping, with the cuts spaced closer together than on gentler curves.

Squaring Up

When you are creating a quilted project with a layer of batting in between the top and bottom layers, you will need to ensure that all layers are flush around the edges before you finish the edges (usually by binding them).

Place your quilt onto a self-healing mat and square up the edges by using a metal yardstick or a rigid clear acrylic ruler and rotary cutter to trim each edge as necessary so that all layers are even and the corners form neat right angles. Use the edge of the ruler as a guide to make straight cuts with the rotary cutter.

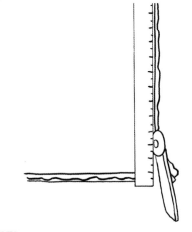

PATTERN GUIDE

Here is a quick reference guide to the symbols and markings on the patterns, as well as brief instructions on using patterns.

Using the Pattern Insert:

Although you can simply cut the patterns directly from the pattern insert, you'll probably want to leave it intact because some of the the patterns overlap each other. Instead, trace the selected pattern onto Swedish tracing paper (see Resources on p. 158) or other pattern paper (such as butcher paper or newsprint) and cut out. Then you can either pin the pattern pieces to the fabric and cut around them or trace the pattern pieces onto the fabric with a fabric marking pen or tailor's chalk and then cut out along the traced lines. Be sure to pin or transfer the pattern pieces to the wrong side (p. 153) of the fabric, as well as to transfer all pattern markings.

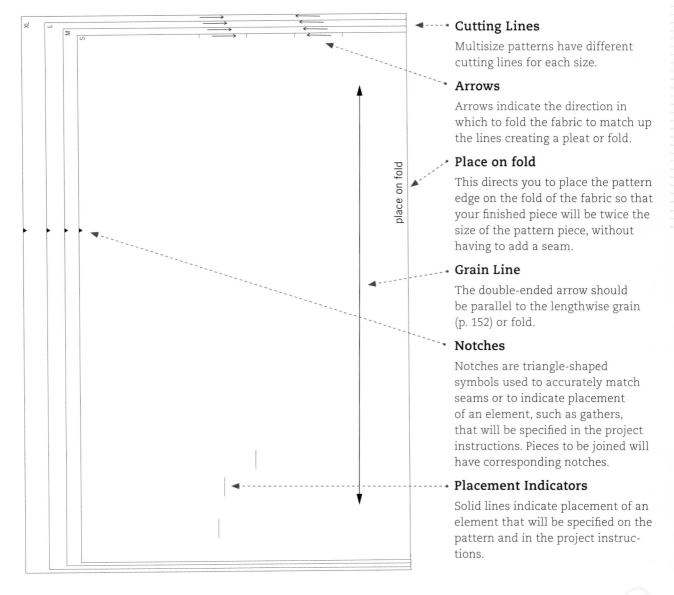

Cutting Lines

Multisize patterns have different cutting lines for each size.

Arrows

Arrows indicate the direction in which to fold the fabric to match up the lines creating a pleat or fold.

Place on fold

This directs you to place the pattern edge on the fold of the fabric so that your finished piece will be twice the size of the pattern piece, without having to add a seam.

Grain Line

The double-ended arrow should be parallel to the lengthwise grain (p. 152) or fold.

Notches

Notches are triangle-shaped symbols used to accurately match seams or to indicate placement of an element, such as gathers, that will be specified in the project instructions. Pieces to be joined will have corresponding notches.

Placement Indicators

Solid lines indicate placement of an element that will be specified on the pattern and in the project instructions.

RESOURCES

There is almost nothing that I love more than walking into a local fabric store and touching everything I can get my hands on. Be sure to visit your local fabric and/or quilt stores for materials and inspiration. There are also many online retailers offering a variety of supplies. Here, I share with you some of my favorite resources for fabric, notions, and creative inspiration.

FABRIC, NOTIONS, AND SUPPLIES

Blick Art Materials

PO Box 1267
Galesburg, IL 61402-1267
(800) 723-2787
dickblick.com

Saral wax transfer paper for embroidery design transfer and self-adhesive mounting board

Crafter's Market

PO Box 15565
Chesapeake, VA 23328
(757) 546-0364
craftersmarket.net

Self-stick needlework mounting board

Etsy

etsy.com

Hard-to-find Japanese fabrics and other specialty fabrics

Hancock's of Paducah

(800) 845-8723
hancocks-paducah.com

Freezer paper and jelly rolls

Jo-Ann Fabric and Craft Stores

(888) 739-4120
joann.com

Velveteen, wool suiting, corduroy, template plastic, and other appliqué supplies

NearSea Naturals

PO Box 345
Rowe, NM 87562
(877) 573-2913
nearseanaturals.com

Organic fabrics, wool flannel, and Swedish tracing paper for tracing patterns

Purl Patchwork

147 Sullivan St.
New York, NY 10012
(212) 420-8798
purlsoho.com

Cotton, cotton/linen blends, and notions

Strapworks.com

(541) 741-0658
strapworks.com

Slide adjusters and parachute clasps

1 Stop Square

9105 Anthony Ln.
Spring Grove, IL 60081
(815) 675-2751
1stopsquare.com

Craft punches and circle/hole cutters

WOOL FELT

Felt-o-rama

9716-B Rea Rd. #150
Charlotte, NC 28277
feltorama.com

Soft wool-blend felt

Magic Cabin

PO Box 1049
Madison, VA 22727
(888) 623-3655
magiccabin.com

100% wool felt

Prairie Point Junction's Wool Felt Central

Prairie Point Junction Quilt Shop
124 East 8th St., PO Box 184
Cozad, NE 69130
(308) 784-2010
woolfeltcentral.com

Thick, sturdy wool-blend felt

INSPIRATIONAL MAGAZINES

Stitch

201 E. Fourth St.
Loveland, CO 80537
quiltingarts.com/STITCH

Living Crafts

(866) 706-7323
livingcrafts.com

Mothering Magazine

PO Box 1690
Santa Fe, NM 87504
(505) 984-8116
mothering.com

INSPIRATIONAL BLOGS

angrychicken.typepad.com

checkoutgirlcrafts.blogspot.com

mayamade.blogspot.com

oneprettything.com

purlbee.com

rosylittlethings.typepad.com

sewmamasew.com/blog2

soulemama.com

whipup.net

INDEX

CREATE BEAUTIFUL PIECES

WITH THESE INSPIRING RESOURCES FROM INTERWEAVE

I Love Patchwork
*21 Irresistible
Zakka Projects to Sew*
Rashida Coleman-Hale
$24.95
ISBN 978-1-59668-142-2

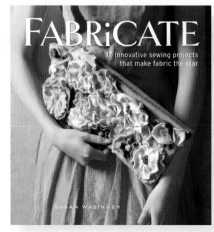

Fabricate
*17 Innovative Sewing Projects
That Make Fabric the Star*
Susan Wasinger
$22.95
ISBN 978-1-59668-094-4

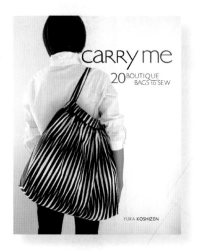

Carry Me
20 Boutique Bags to Sew
Yuka Koshizen
$19.95
ISBN 978-1-59668-184-2

Quilting Arts
MAGAZINE®

Whether you consider yourself a contemporary quilter, fiber artist, art quilter, embellished quilter, or wearable-art artist, *Quilting Arts* strives to meet your creative needs.

quiltingarts.com